Edilson Chaves de Freitas

The effects of revising or cancelling a binding precedent

Edilson Chaves de Freitas

The effects of revising or cancelling a binding precedent

ScienciaScripts

Imprint

Cover image: www.ingimage.com

This book is a translation from the original published under ISBN 978-620-2-04044-0.

Publisher:
Sciencia Scripts
is a trademark of
Dodo Books Indian Ocean Ltd. and OmniScriptum S.R.L publishing group

120 High Road, East Finchley, London, N2 9ED, United Kingdom
Str. Armeneasca 28/1, office 1, Chisinau MD-2012, Republic of Moldova, Europe
Managing Directors: Ieva Konstantinova, Victoria Ursu
info@omniscriptum.com

Printed at: see last page
ISBN: 978-620-8-52340-4

Edilson Chaves de Freitas

Bachelor's Degree in Law and Accounting from the Federal University of Campina Grande - UFCG. Postgraduate degree in Civil Procedural Law from the Federal University of Campina Grande - UFCG. Post-graduate degree in Community Policing, with a specialization in Public Security from the Universidade do Sul de Santa Catarina - UNISUL. Substitute Judge of the Court of Justice of the State of Rio Grande do Norte. Visiting Professor on the Postgraduate Course in Criminology, Criminal Law and Criminal Procedure at the University of Quixeramobim - UNIQ. Lecturer. Former Substitute Judge of the Court of Justice of the State of Ceara. Former Judge of the Court of Justice of the State of Piaui. He was a Civil Police Delegate in the State of Rio Grande do Norte, Legal Advisor to the Court of Auditors of the State of Piaui, Technical Consultant to the President of the Court of Auditors of the State of Piaui, Lawyer and Investigation Agent for the Civil Police of the State of Paraiba.

The Sumula Vinculante and the effects of its revision or canceled by the STF on the Coisa Julgada.

I dedicate this work to my parents Abraao Manoel Chaves and Nuci Dantas de Freitas Chaves for always supporting me at every moment of my life, to my siblings and friends from college and work.

SUMMARY

SUMMARY

The institute of the relativization of res judicata comes into apparent conflict with the principle of legal certainty. However, other values have been given greater attention, such as the principle of equality and the fairness of decisions. Res judicata suffered a break in the model defended by Liebman, in terms of the effects of the decision, with the emergence of collective actions, such as those based on the Consumer Protection Code and the Statute for Children and Adolescents. Judicial precedents have always been used as a formal source of law in the common law legal system. The basis for respecting precedents, in its origins, was the absence of a legislated rule. Nowadays, English and American law coexists with both legislated law and summarized jurisprudential decisions. The civil law system has moved away from unconditional attachment to the law, giving greater prominence to the consolidated decisions of the courts. The changes undergone by the two systems have led to the emergence of a mixed system, applying both civil law and common law rules. The binding summary, introduced into Brazilian law by constitutional amendment no. 45/2004 and regulated by law no. 11.417/2006 and resolutions no. 381, of October 29, 2008 and no. 388, of December 5, 2008, has a mixed legal nature. It is a jurisdictional act because it originates from repeated decisions on the same specific case. It is akin to a normative act because it is general in nature and must be complied with by the bodies of the judiciary and the direct and indirect public administration. The binding summula differs from the summula impeditiva de recuso in terms of its recipients. While the former is intended to compel the judge to apply the understanding summarized by the Federal Supreme Court, the latter is intended for the losing party in the case who expresses a desire to appeal. When it deals with constitutional matters, the binding summary is similar in its effects (erga omnes and ex tunc) to the direct action of constitutionality/declaratory action of constitutionality. Once a court has ruled that a provision of law is unconstitutional, it cannot then revise the ruling, just as it is not possible for a rule declared unconstitutional in concentrated control to be submitted to a declaratory action for constitutionality. The number of people entitled to propose the creation, revision or cancellation of a summary was expanded by Law 11.417/2006, with the aim of avoiding the plastering of summarized understandings. The revision or cancellation of a summary should be treated differently depending on the rule it interprets (constitutional or infra-constitutional rule). The research was problematized by the fact that the legislator regulates the matter without defining the scope of the revision or cancellation of binding precedents for res judicata. The objectives are to identify how res judicata sentences behave in the face of changes to the binding summa. The study was carried out using a deductive approach, with comparative and interpretative procedures, based on bibliographical research consisting mainly of books and scientific articles, which provide the researcher with subsidies to properly understand the consequences of revising or canceling the binding summa.

Key words: Sumula Vinculante. Res judicata. Binding effect.

INTRODUCTION

The purpose of this work is to analyze some of the institutes of res judicata and their counterpoint with the effects of its revision or cancellation on res judicata, in the light of Constitutional Amendment n. 45/2004, Law n. 11.417/2006, doctrine and Brazilian case law.

The problematization of the research is based on the fact that the legislator regulates the matter without defining the scope of the review or cancellation of a binding summary for res judicata. The study will be carried out using a deductive approach, with comparative and interpretative procedures, based on bibliographical research in books, magazines and relevant articles.

The first step will be to make a conceptual analysis of the institute of res judicata based on classical doctrine and its practical implications in the face of the recent trend towards the relativization of res judicata. An analysis will be made of the historical evolution of the concept of res judicata from the classical conceptions of Liebman and Chiovenda to the current conceptions put forward by modern doctrine, such as Barbosa Moreira. It goes on to discuss the distinctions between formal res judicata, preclusion and material res judicata, as well as their consequences inside and outside the process.

After establishing the notion of the institute, we will move on to consider the implications of the control of the constitutionality of norms in the face of res judicata, emphasizing the divergence of doctrine and jurisprudence, including that of the higher courts, regarding the deconstitution of res judicata. The changes that have occurred in the process of enforcing sentences, through the reform of the Code of Civil Procedure in 2005, will be analyzed, making it possible to allege the nullity of a sentence that was based on a law that was later declared unconstitutional, even though the decision in the knowledge phase has become final.

It will then deal with res judicata in relation to continuing relationships and in the collective sphere. Doctrinal discussion will be brought up regarding continuing relationships as an instrument characterizing a new fact for the second process and not as a basis for relativizing res judicata. The extension of res judicata in the collective sphere aims to reach people who did not take part in the procedural relationship, as long as the outcome of the judgment is favorable.

An examination will also be made of the institute of relativization of res judicata in relation to the principles of legal certainty and the fairness of decisions. Proponents of the fairness of decisions openly accept the deconstruction of a final judgment, even if the time limit for rescission provided for in the Code of Civil Procedure has already passed, such as Humberto Theodoro Junior. Those who deny the rescission of unjust judgments claim that it would be more unjust to reform a judgment covered by the cloak of res judicata. The truth is that legal certainty has been mitigated by Brazilian doctrine and jurisprudence, as will be clear from reading the first chapter.

The second chapter will analyze the inclusion of binding precedents in Brazilian law. But first, we will try to examine the behavior of judicial precedents in the common law and civil law legal systems. In the analysis of the common law system, judicial precedents in English and American law will be studied and how they contributed to the creation of the binding precedent in Brazilian law. This will be followed by a study of the Roman-Germanic system, the basis of traditional Brazilian law. From the analysis of the two systems, considerations will be made about the emergence of a mixed system in the light of the globalization of legal norms.

In continuation of the work, the nature of the binding summula inserted into the Brazilian legal system by constitutional amendment n. 45/2004 will be analyzed, noting that depending on how it is received (judicial or normative), the repercussions for res judicata will be different.

With the aim of clarifying the institute of the binding summary, its regulation by the Federal Constitution, by Law 11.417/2006 and by Resolutions 381 of October 29, 2008 and 388 of December 5, 2008, both of the Federal Supreme Court, will be addressed. It will be shown that the procedure for issuing, reviewing and canceling binding precedents is not sufficiently disciplined and could lead to serious inconveniences in the future.

The behavior of res judicata in the face of the institute of binding precedents will be examined. In defense of the equality of all before the law and the judiciary, it will be seen that the change in orientation with regard to res judicata aims to give equal rights to all situations.

We will also discuss the ambitious intention of the constituent assembly when it tried to insert the sumula impeditiva de recursos alongside the sumula vinculante in the judicial reform project. It will be seen that the bill was unsuccessful in getting the final text approved. The ordinary legislator subsequently regulated the matter in the Civil Procedure Code in such a timid way that it is incapable of producing concrete results.

The last chapter will seek to demonstrate the consequences of revising or canceling the binding summa for res judicata. To this end, a comparative study will be made of the direct action of unconstitutionality and the declaratory action of constitutionality with the binding summary. With the aim of equalizing the institutes, the reforming constituent tried to regulate the effect of the three supports in the same provision of the Constitution, but was unsuccessful when the final text was approved. It will be analyzed whether this separation is intended to give differentiated treatment or whether it was done in order to better adapt topographically.

In continuation of the study, questions will be asked about the appropriateness of the rescission action to annul a previous judgment that disrespected res judicata. To this end, it will bring up arguments for and against, such as that of Osmar Mendes, who believes that it is not possible to use the rescission procedure to overturn a final judgment.

With regard to the procedure for reviewing and canceling a binding summa, the aim is to give an overview of the legal entities involved, the quorum required for review/cancellation, whether or not it is possible to suspend the proceedings during the review process, and the role of third parties, among others.

Finally, the consequences of revising or canceling a summary for res judicata will be studied. To this end, we will separate the summaries that deal with constitutional matters from those that deal with rules of a different nature. With regard to the former, we will discuss the possibility of review when the summary declares the unconstitutionality of a provision of law, given that they are equivalent to a direct action for unconstitutionality. In the other cases, it will be analyzed when the revision or cancellation will take effect, whether *ex tunc* or *ex nunc*.

CHAPTER 1: RELATIVIZATION OF THE COURT AND LEGAL SECURITY

Res judicata has always deserved special protection from the state, which is concerned with the stability of decisions handed down by judicial bodies. The finality of decisions represents the recognition of jurisdiction, since it was created to put an end to litigation. Marinoni's guidance (2008, p. 5960) in defense of the stability of decisions is clear, *verbis*:

> If conflicts, once resolved, could be re-discussed, or if the judge's solution could be denied, there would be no point in jurisdiction. So the court's decision becomes immutable and indisputable.
> In fact, the decision produced in the state process is not final just because it puts an end to an argument and prevents the reopening of litigation, but because it constitutes the firming up of state power.

However, modern doctrine and case law have made the effects of res judicata more flexible. According to Osmar Mendes (2008, p. 71), this approach allows: "certain situations already recrudesced, or covered by the cloak of res judicata, could, for reasons of justification mainly, even if outside the decadence period for filing the rescission action, be modified or revised".

1.1 Preliminary notes on res judicata

Initially, it is worth making some procedural considerations about res judicata, with a view to demonstrating its practical implications in the Brazilian legal system, in relation to the parties and third parties.

Andre Ramos (2007, p. 21) summarizes the concept of res judicata precisely:

> Res judicata is the legal-procedural institute created with the aim of giving judicial decisions a necessary stability, embodied in the impossibility of changing their content. As Candido Dinamarco states, "in procedural law, res judicata is immutability". It is therefore directly linked to the idea of security.

The doctrine, when conceptualizing res judicata, always seeks to relate this institute to legal certainty. The two institutes go towards the same goal, which is to give legal certainty.

stability of judicial decisions. In the same vein are the words of Cassiano Luiz (2008, p. 31), guided by Chiovenda, in the following terms:

> Chiovenda also defined res judicata as "the indisputable and obligatory affirmation by judges in all future proceedings of a concrete will of the law, which recognizes or denies a good of life to one of the parties": from this comes to form the concept of res judicata the content of the judgment (affirmation of a will of the law), its effect (obligatory) and finally a quality of this (indisputability).

The Constitution of the Republic did not define res judicata. It confined itself to saying, in Article 5, XXXVI, that the law shall not prejudice res judicata. The original legislator did the right thing, because it is not his job to create concepts. Creating concepts is the job of the ordinary legislator, the courts and the doctrine. The Introductory Law to the Civil Code defines res judicata, in art. 6, § 3, as being "a judicial decision against which there can no longer be an appeal". The Code of Civil Procedure, in Article 467, defines res judicata as "the effectiveness that renders a judgment immutable and indisputable, no longer subject to ordinary or extraordinary appeal." This concept receives a lot of criticism from national doctrine, due to its imprecision and deficiency. In this sense are the words of Andre Ramos (2007, p. 24), *verbis:*

> The truth is that the Civil Procedure Code, in trying to establish the concept of res judicata in the aforementioned provision, was unfortunate, as it implies that res judicata is formed when there is no further appeal against any *judgment*. It will be seen below that this statement is mistaken, when the proper distinctions are made between res *judicata* and *formal res judicata*.
> (...)
> Therefore, as the definition given by the Civil Procedure Code for res judicata is imprecise and deficient, and is disallowed by other provisions of the code itself, as demonstrated, the fact that it has moved away from the Liebmanian theory does not prevent us from adopting it here. After all, it cannot be denied that Liebman's theory is widely dominant in Portuguese doctrine, which is why it will be adopted in this work.

It is worth highlighting Barbosa Moreira's criticism of Liebman's concept of res judicata. He argues that res judicata does not make the effects of the judgment immutable, but rather the content of the command it contains. Andre Ramos (2007, p. 25) states that the criticism of Liebman is pertinent in the sense of making amends for the synthetic concept:

> The criticism is pertinent, but as long as we only take into account the pure and simple concept given by Liebman to the institute, which in fact refers to res judicata as *the quality of the effects of a judgment, making them immutable and indisputable.* However, if we analyze

the work of the Italian master, we will see that, as Eduardo Talamini himself points out, "Barbosa Moreira's criticism is more a repair to the synthetic formula of Liebman's thesis ('res judicata and the quality of the effects') than an opposition to the content of Liebman's theory as a whole".

Therefore, the concepts of the distinguished proceduralists converge on the same point, with Barbosa Moreira being more analytical. The truth is that the Italian master's concept is fundamental to solving the most varied problems linked to res judicata. Candido Dinamarco (2003, p. 304) goes so far as to say that Liebman's theory "is one of the most elegant achievements of procedural science in the century of procedural enlightenment".

1.2 Distinction between formal res judicata and material res judicata

The difference between formal res judicata and substantive res judicata is clear. Aware of the importance of this distinction for this work, it is worth explaining it first. The Code of Civil Procedure limits itself to defining res judicata. But the doctrine recognizes the existence of formal res judicata, traditionally treated by proceduralists as a relevant fact in terms of the effectiveness of the sentence. Humberto Theodoro (2004, p. 482) states that the difference between the two "is only one of degree of the same phenomenon. Both stem from the impossibility of lodging an appeal against the judgment."

Seeking to draw a parallel between the two institutes, Cassiano Luiz (2008, p. 30) states that:

> Formal res judicata would be a lesser degree of stability of the effects of the judgment, i.e. it would occur when all the appeals available in a given case have been exhausted and the judgment can no longer be challenged in the same procedural relationship.

In accordance with Cassiano and Eduardo Talamini's link, quoted by Andre Luiz (2007, p. 26), *verbis:*

> It should be noted that res judicata and res judicata are unmistakable institutes. It was canon law that made the distinction. If, on the one hand, there is no res judicata without res judicata, on the other hand, res judicata does not always bring with it material res judicata. At most, res judicata can be linked to formal res judicata (...). But even so, the two concepts are not identical. The first concerns the chronological aspect of the exhaustion of internal means of reviewing the judgment; the second concerns the authority that is established, preventing the reopening of proceedings. They are in a cause and effect relationship.

For Leibman and his followers, such as Candido Rangel Dinamarco, *apud*

Andre Luiz (2007, p.27), formal and material res judicata are not autonomous institutes, but two aspects of the same phenomenon of immutability, both related to legal certainty. In fact, they represent two sides of the same coin, two different manifestations of the same and unique legal phenomenon.

Formal res judicata derives from the immutability of the judgment within the proceedings in which it was handed down due to the impossibility of filing an appeal. This impossibility results from the fact that the party has already used up all the appeals, or has exhausted the time limit stipulated by law, or has given up the appeal or waived it. Formal res judicata acts within the proceedings in which the judgment was handed down, without preventing the subject matter of the judgment from being discussed again in other proceedings (THEODORO, 2004).

Andre Luiz (2007, p. 27), after stating that there is a direct relationship between formal res judicata and procedural estoppel, divides the latter into three types, as follows:

> According to procedural doctrine, there are basically three types of estoppel: *temporal,* which stems from the loss of the deadline - or the appropriate procedural phase - for exercising a certain procedural power or faculty; *consumptive*, which stems from the previous exercise of the procedural power or faculty during the course of the proceedings; and *logical,* which stems from the practice of an act that is logically incompatible with the practice of another certain power or faculty.

The loss of the right to appeal can be manifested in three ways: by the expiry of the time limit, by the performance of an act incompatible with the desire to appeal and by the filing of the appeal. These three forms represent, respectively, the three types of estoppel described above. Therefore, formal res judicata and estoppel have effects restricted to the proceedings in which they occurred. Both have the function of ensuring the indisputability of crystallized legal situations endoprocessually.

Jose Maria Tesheiner *apud* Andre Luiz (2007, 28) makes a fine distinction between formal res judicata and estoppel, *verbis:*

> The judgment, no longer subject to appeal, formally becomes final. Immutability is restricted to the proceedings in which the judgment was handed down. If the appropriate appeal has not been lodged, the judgment formally becomes res judicata and can no longer be modified, in the same proceedings, for the simple reason that it has been extinguished.
> With regard to interlocutory decisions, which are unchangeable and indisputable in the proceedings in which they were handed down, it is said that there is *preclusion, while* the expression *formal res judicata* is reserved for sentences.

In this way, it can be said that formal res judicata is preclusion at its highest level, since it prevents the judgment from being reissued in the same case. Material res judicata is the extrinsic security of the process. The content of the judgment becomes immutable both inside and outside the proceedings, and even affects administrative and legislative authorities. It is not limited to the judgment as a procedural act. It goes further, reaching the substantial effects of the judgment. The words of Jose Maria Tesheiner, *apud* Andre Luiz (2007, p. 29), are precise:

> Every judgment produces formal res judicata from the moment it becomes unappealable. However, not every judgment produces material res judicata. For material res judicata to occur, the content of the judgment must not be disregarded or modified, even in another proceeding or in another action, with the exception of rescission, which is intended precisely to deconstruct material res judicata.

1.3 Res judicata and constitutionality control

Constitutionality control consists of a mechanism through which the constitutionally competent body exercises control over normative acts, verifying their adequacy to the precepts of the constitutional norm. In Brazil, the body authorized to exercise concentrated control is the Federal Supreme Court, but each judge, when judging a specific case, exercises abstract control of norms. This control is typical of countries with a rigid constitution, such as Brazil. Alexandre de Morais states that:

> The idea of the intersection between constitutionality control and rigid constitutions is such that in a state where there is no constitutionality control, the constitution will be flexible, even if it is called rigid, because the unlimited constituent power will be in the hands of the ordinary legislator.

The decision of the Federal Supreme Court declaring a law unconstitutional, in the concentrated control of constitutionality, is effective for the past or *ex tunc*. Doctrine differs as to whether the decision affects final and unappealable judgments based on the law declared unconstitutional. Marinoni (2008, p. 25), after warning that foreign legislation has made reservations to the doctrine of non-retroactivity, such as Australia, states that *ex tunc* effectiveness does not affect all past situations, *verbis:*

> It should also be pointed out that the retroactive effect of a decision of unconstitutionality does not concern the control of the constitutionality of judicial decisions, but only the control of the constitutionality of laws. Although this is obvious in principle, the thesis of the retroactivity of

the decision of unconstitutionality on res judicata often forgets that in this hypothesis we are dealing with the control of the constitutionality of the law, and not a means of controlling the constitutionality of judicial decisions.

The opinion of the doctor cited above seems to be in the minority. Once the unconstitutionality of the law that served as the basis for the judgment has been declared, the judgment will be compromised by logical imperative. The unconstitutionality of the decision is the logical consequence of the unconstitutionality of the law.

Marinoni (2008, p. 26), in defending his thesis, criticizes the defenders of the unconstitutionality of judicial decisions, since the Chiovendian theory of jurisdiction is no longer applicable. According to her, the jurisdictional function is to carry out the will of the law. Chiovenda went so far as to say that jurisdiction only manifests itself once the legislator has revealed itself. In the words of Marinoni (2008, p. 27), "one cannot confuse the application of the general rule to the specific case with the creation of the individual rule of the specific case." The law is not just the creation of the legislator. The judge also creates the law when he judges the specific case, even when applying the general rule.

When judging a concrete case, the judge has the power to control its constitutionality. Once the judge has carried out the control, according to Marinoni (2008, p. 32), there can be no further review:

> A judgment that has become res judicata, since it is a rule drawn up by a judge who has a duty to carry out diffuse control of constitutionality, cannot be invalidated because it was based on a law that was later declared unconstitutional. It should be noted that this would amount to the nullification *of* the *constitutionality judgment,* and not just the nullification of the law declared unconstitutional. Preventing the law declared unconstitutional from taking effect is very different from denying effect to a constitutionality judgment, legitimized by the Constitution itself.

Following the above understanding, Osmar Mendes Paixao (2008, p.85) says that a final and unappealable decision cannot be overturned simply because it disagrees with the Supreme Court's current dominant case law.
According to him, "legal certainty must prevail and res judicata must be respected, even if it is criticized as unfair and contrary to equal treatment, otherwise social relations will become unstable."

The opinion of these distinguished scholars that a final judgment based on an unconstitutional law is untouchable should not be upheld.

The hierarchical-normative superiority of the Constitution means that each and every act emanating from public power must be subject to it, under penalty of invalidity. According to Andre Luiz (2007, p. 95), each and every act must comply with the Constitution in order to be valid. In his words (2007, p. 95):

> This is important since, as Humberto Theodoro Junior observes - quoting Paulo Otero's liposophies - in the area of unconstitutionality, for a long time the attention and concern of jurists was focused on examining the constitutional non-conformity of legislative acts, which contributed to the institutionalization of the myth of the impermeability of res judicata court decisions, even if they contained defects of unconstitutionality.

The reason is undoubtedly with the doctrine that argues that unconstitutional res judicata is subject to rescission. To think otherwise would be to restrict the meaning of Article 485, V of the Code of Civil Procedure too much. This is the opinion of Andre Luiz (2007, p. 101), *verbis*:

> We have already pointed out that the rescission action based on Article 485(V) of the Code of Civil Procedure can be used to correct unconstitutionalities that may affect judgments covered by res judicata. This is because the expression *law* used in the normative provision in question must be understood in a very broad way. Furthermore, it would be completely inconsistent to allow the review of *illegal* judgments and not allow the same for *unconstitutional* judgments.

The Federal Supreme Court believes that when a judgment violates the Constitution, Sumula n. 343 does not apply[1] . In other words, even if the matter is controversial in the courts, once the STF has ruled that it is unconstitutional, the final judgment must be rescinded. The words of Reporting Justice Gilmar Mendes in the judgment of RE 328.812 AM are precise:

> As noted by Walter Burckhardt, what is identified as the will of the Constitution 'must be honestly preserved, even if, to do so, we have to renounce some benefits, or even some just advantages. Anyone who is willing to sacrifice an interest for the sake of preserving a constitutional principle strengthens respect for the Constitution and guarantees a good in life that is indispensable to the essence of the state, especially the democratic state'. Those who, on the other hand, are unwilling to make this sacrifice, 'gradually squander a capital which means much more than all the advantages gained, and which, if wasted, will never be recovered. (A Forga Normativa da Constituigao, Porto Alegre: Sergio Antonio Fabris Editor, 1991, p. 21-22).
>
> The application of Sumula 343 in constitutional matters is an affront not only to the normative force of the Constitution, but also to the principle of maximum effectiveness of the constitutional norm. Admitting the application of the guidance contained in the aforementioned entry in matters of constitutional interpretation means strengthening the decisions of the

[1] Sumula 343: An action for rescission for an offense against a literal provision of law does not lie when the rescinding decision is based on a legal text whose interpretation is controversial in the courts.

ordinary courts to the detriment of the decisions of the Federal Supreme Court. This practice is all the more serious considering that in our general system of constitutionality control, the STF's voice will only be heard after years of dealing with issues in two ordinary instances. Favoring controversial interpretations in order to maintain judgments that go against the Court's guidance means affronting the effectiveness of the Constitution. (RAMOS, 2007, P. 107)

This decision is the result of the relativization of the institute of res judicata, as will be studied in more detail in the following sections.

1.4 The declaration of unconstitutionality as an obstacle to the enforcement of a final judgment

The ordinary legislator, following the guidance of the majority of legal scholars, has been expanding the situations in which a final judgment can be reformed. An example of this is the insertion of a single paragraph to art. 741 by provisional measure n. 2.180-35/2001 and of § 1 to art. 475-L by law n. 11.232/2005 in the Civil Procedure Code. These provisions equate an unenforceable judicial title with one based on a law or normative act declared unconstitutional by the Federal Supreme Court, or based on an application or interpretation of the law or normative act considered by the Supreme Court to be incompatible with the constitution.

The expansion of the deconstruction of res judicata has only been possible thanks to the work of authors Humberto Theodoro Junior, Juliana Cordeiro de Farias and Jose Delgado. It is also worth highlighting the work of Gilmar Mendes, when he was in charge of the Federal Attorney General's Office, through seminars promoted by this institution.

Marinoni, a defender of res judicata, denies the relativization of the institute. He claims that art. 475-L, like art. 485 of the CPC, merely confirms the rule, since they are exceptions. In his words (2008, p. 122), *verbis:*

Res judicata remedies any defects and nullities that may have existed in the process, and with its formation, any allegation that the defendant may have presented can no longer be brought before the Judiciary to hinder the realization of the right (art. 474 of the CPC). The exceptions are cases of rescission (art. 485 of the CPC), situations of procedural non-existence *(querela nullitatis)* and the aforementioned hypotheses listed in art. 475-L.

The author criticizes the inclusion of art. 475-L in Brazilian legislation. The rule transplanted from German law does not fit in with Brazilian reality. In Germany, the ordinary judge has no jurisdiction to deal with constitutional issues. In Brazil, according to the author, the situation is quite different, as each and every judge has the duty to carry out constitutionality control, via the diffuse route, when judging a specific case.

But Marinoni's orientation is in the minority. The majority view is that the unenforceability of a court order based on a law that has been declared unconstitutional is a clear example of the relativization of res judicata. The allegation has only been anticipated, insofar as it is being allowed to challenge its enforceability in the context of a motion to stay execution, i.e. independently of the rescission action.

The major discussion in the preliminary draft that gave rise to the sole paragraph of article 741 of the CPC concerned the scope of the decision of unconstitutionality of the STF. Part of the doctrine took the view that it should only cover cases in which the STF's decision on the (in)constitutionality of the rule was taken in a direct action, i.e. in an objective process of concentrated control of constitutionality. However, the prevailing view, led by Humberto Theodoro, won the day, and the embargo was applicable both when the judgment went against the decision of the Supreme Court in concentrated control and in diffuse control.

1.5 Res judicata and continuing relationships

The preclusive effect of res judicata renders indisputable the allegations linked to the claim, the parties and the cause of action debated in the case. In the case of continuing legal relationships, provided for in article 471, I, of the Code of Civil Procedure, the new judicial assessment is based on a change in the state of fact or law of the previous claim. A final judgment is re-examined due to a new fact caused by a change in the circumstances surrounding the parties. The words of Andre Luiz (2007, p. 41) are precise, *verbis*:

> It must be made clear that the article in question does not mean that res judicata is not formed in continuing legal relationships. In these relationships, res judicata occurs normally, as in any other legal relationship. However, because it refers to a legal situation that is constantly changing even after the final *decision has been made*, it is exceptionally permissible for one of the parties to ask the court to review what has been decided. Liebman himself, in his classic study, referred to the problem.

The issue is similar to the hypothesis of the supervening of a new fact. The only difference is that the new fact that gives rise to the new cause of action arises from the dynamism of the continuing legal relationship and arises in the course of the relationship itself.

According to Marinoni (2008, p. 142), the res judicata imposed on the first decision is not affected, because the factual or legal changes give rise to a new cause of action, creating a new action that is totally different from the previous one. The issue decided in the second action arises from new circumstances not addressed in the previous action. Nor can it be said that a judgment that decides on continuing relationships, such as a maintenance judgment, does not become final or res judicata. With regard to maintenance, a change in the financial situation of one of the parties is a subsequent circumstance that gives rise to a new cause of action and produces a new res judicata, without excluding the res judicata of the previous judgment. In the words of Marinoni (2008, p. 142):

> A change in the factual circumstances constitutes a change in the cause of action, forming another (new) action and giving rise to another (new) res judicata. Thus, when the factual circumstances change, another (new) res judicata will be formed, which must coexist in harmony with the res judicata regarding the previous circumstances.

A curious aspect is the modification of the law as a basis for bringing a new action when the legal relationship is ongoing. For example, a new law comes into force which does not recognize the relationship between the grandchild and the grandparent, thus removing the obligation to pay maintenance. In this case, the judgment that recognized the right to maintenance based on the previous law, even though it has become final, will suffer the effects of the new law. The plaintiff can file a new lawsuit claiming that the law after the judgment is a new circumstance.

A judgment handed down under the old law cannot continue to produce effects after the change in the legal system. According to Marinoni (2008, p. 144), to think otherwise would be to disregard the effects of new laws on ongoing relationships. In his words:

> It should be noted that considering a new law, as well as a new fact, is simply admitting the existence of continuing relationships. In fact, the realization that a new law can put an end to a benefit hitherto granted by res judicata is a reflection of the markedly temporal structure of the law itself.

The judge must be careful not to accept an old circumstance in the guise of a new circumstance in the new lawsuit. Sometimes, the plaintiff wants to re-litigate the case on the basis of elements that pre-existed the first case. In this case, it cannot be said that there has been a change in the state of fact or law to invoke article 471, I, of the Code of Civil Procedure. A distinction must be made between circumstances that change (temporary elements) and circumstances that remain the same (perennial or stable elements).

1.6 Res judicata in the collective sphere

With the evolution of the individual state to the social state, there was a need to effectively protect second and third generation rights (environment, consumer rights, administrative morality), which originated in mass relations, relativizing the absolute character that individual rights, characterized as first generation, once enjoyed.

Collective actions, like those provided for in the Consumer Protection Code, have given a new normative orientation to the institute of res judicata. It is possible to subjectively extend the effects of the decision, when it is favorable to the plaintiffs. If the claim is dismissed, individual rights continue to be protected.

There has been a real expansion of access to justice, representing a real advance in citizens' rights. This change requires flexibility in the traditional institutes of res judicata to meet the peculiarities of this new type of claim. Cassiano Luiz (2008, p. 42) says that "in collective claims, the subjective extension of the authority of res judicata was provided for, partially breaking with the classical doctrine that did not allow the judgment to reach those who were not technically a party".

The extension of the effects of res judicata to third parties depends on the nature of the judgment, in other words, it is *secundo eventum litis.* In this sense, it is worth transcribing a few words from Cassiano Luiz (2008, p. 43):

> Thus, the protection of the values set out in collective actions implies that: a) res judicata does not occur in the event of an unfavorable judgment, if this occurred due to insufficient evidence; b) res judicata operates exclusively at the level of the collective civil action, in other words, it does not affect individual rights, except in the case of article 94 with article 102, paragraph 2 of the Consumer Protection Code, which will be explained below; c) the subjective scope of the judgment corresponds directly to the class of beneficiaries, whether the legal relationship covers diffuse, collective or homogeneous individual rights.

Thus, it has been shown that the res judicata disciplined by the Consumer Protection Code differs from the traditional application of the Civil Procedure Code, in terms of the extension of the subjective effects of the claim, since the effectiveness of the judgment does not only affect the parties to the case.

1.7 The relativization of res judicata as a reflection of the tension between the values of legal certainty and justice

Res judicata is directly related to legal certainty, the latter being the main foundation for its establishment. The principle of legal certainty is divided into two aspects, one objective and the other subjective. Objectively, legal certainty manifests itself as a demand for the regularity of the legal system through its rules and institutions. In other words, it represents the guarantee of obedience to the process of drawing up rules and the perpetuity of the institutions that make up a legal system.

On the subjective side, legal certainty is presented as certainty of law, or rather, as the protection of objective certainty in personal situations.

The words of Andre Luiz (2007, p.48) regarding the extension of the term legal certainty are very precise, *verbis:*

> It is well established that legal certainty is a general principle of law, which appears in the most varied branches of the legal tree. In criminal law, for example, legal certainty clearly appears in the prohibition of the retroactivity of the law (with the well-known exception of *lex mitior)* and in the prohibition of the analogical application of incriminating criminal law.

Legal certainty is related to the certainty of the law. It is impossible to think of a democratic state without stability in the decisions of the bodies responsible for jurisdiction. The procedural institute that ensures the fulfillment of this state duty and guarantees the satisfaction of this right is, precisely, res judicata. Without it, as has been said, legal-procedural relations would go on forever and insecurity would reign.

Emphasizing the importance of legal certainty for the process, Andre Luiz (2007, p.50) goes so far as to say that "if the procedural legal relationship does not culminate in the formation of a res judicata, the process is only a procedure."

Currently, legal certainty is being mitigated by doctrine and case law. Modern law is undergoing a paradigm shift, with the value of justice taking precedence over the value of security. The words of Andre Luiz (2007, p. 54) regarding the paradigm shift in the modern Democratic State of Law are precise, *verbis:*

> Thus, the paradigm shift mentioned above reflects, in general terms, a movement in the law that is clearly concerned with justice, which is why it has been noticed that, gradually, the value of security, once almost recognized as an absolute value, is giving way to other values, such as justice and effectiveness.
> As a result, res judicata, as an institute that provides legal certainty in the process, is also

coming into question. In other words, the absolute intangibility of res judicata, or its "sanctification", is being criticized. Finally, a "relativization" of *res judicata* is proposed, reflecting the need to make other values prevail over the security that justifies it, among which justice stands out. If legal positivism, in the words of its critics, replaces law as a demand for justice with law as controlled arbitrariness, "res judicata would be nothing but *uncontrolled final arbitrariness"*.

But the definition of justice is very controversial in the doctrine. Hans Kelsen, in "What is Justice", already recognized that there was no exclusive standard of justice.

According to him, *apud* Osmar Mendes (2008, p.19) "what we actually find are many different ideals". He concludes that "the norms of positive law correspond to a certain social reality, but not the norms of justice".

No matter how perfect the system created by the law is in terms of justice, when it is applied it will be imperfect and unjust, because the system is applied by men and they are, by nature, imperfect. On this subject, Andre Luiz (2007, p. 56) concludes that it is not possible to guarantee justice for all outcomes. According to him: "At most, it can be guaranteed that pre-established rules are respected, that mechanisms are provided for the defense of claims and that the decisions taken by the competent bodies are respected".

The conflict between security and justice is as old as law itself. Depending on the historical moment experienced by society, one of them prevails to the detriment of the other. For Andre Luiz (2007, p. 62), the prevalence of certain values in a society will depend, above all, on the historical, political and even economic moment experienced. As for the current situation, his words are conclusive (2007, p. 62), *verbis*:

> In this way, we have tried to highlight the fact that, while for some time legal certainty has prevailed, what we are seeing today is a paradigm shift. In fact, as we said above, modern democratic states of law are characterized by a clear concern for justice, which is why we have noticed that, gradually, the value of security has been losing ground to values such as justice and effectiveness.

Res judicata is an institute intrinsically related to the principle of legal certainty. But legal certainty is not the only objective of civil procedural law. It is on this basis that many modern proceduralists support the need to revise the theory of res judicata, proposing its relativization. It will no longer be possible to preach the almost absolute intangibility of res judicata, as defended by classical doctrine. The law is no longer concerned only with formalism, but with the realization of justice. But the preponderance of one value over another can only be analyzed in a specific case, using the principle of proportionality.

1.8 The relativization of res judicata in Brazilian doctrine and jurisprudence.

In modern times, Brazilian doctrine and jurisprudence have studied the idea of relativizing res judicata, which means making its effects more flexible. Situations covered by the cloak of res judicata could be modified or reviewed, even after the two-year deadline, giving way to the value of justice.

It's worth pointing out, initially, that not all proceduralists agree with the theory of relativizing res judicata. At this point, we will try to present a summary of the arguments for and against the institute of relativization.

One of the first works to defend the relativization of res judicata was the work coordinated by Carlos Valder do Nascimento, in co-authorship with Candido Rangel Dinamarco, Jose Augusto Delgado, Humberto Theodoro Junior and Juliana Cordeiro de Farias (RAMOS, 2008, p. 70). These authors defend the need to review res judicata, even after the deadline for the rescission action has passed.

The proposal to relativize res judicata basically involves cases of decisions that contain intolerable injustices and decisions that are unconstitutional. Doctrine differs as to the grounds for overturning a judgment. For Teresa Wambier and Jose Medina, *apud* Andre Luiz, judgments with these defects are non-existent, *verbis:*

> There are certain judgments, and one of the authors of this essay has been defending this view for a long time, which do not have the capacity to become res judicata. We are dealing here with a group of judgments which we call, according to the terminology we propose, legally existing judgments.

For Humberto Theodoro, *apud* Andre Ramos (2008, p. 72), a judgment that is vitiated by unconstitutionality is null and void in its own right and can be overturned at any time. As you can see, the end result is the same, both for the null sentence and for the non-existent one. What changes is the basis for expunging the final judgment.

Osmar Mendes criticizes Theodoro's view that void sentences can be overturned at any time. For him (2008, p. 73-74), nullity defects are remediable, regardless of whether they are relative or absolute. Once the two-year time limit for the rescission action has elapsed, there is what is known as a general remedy.

Barbosa Moreira, *apud* Andre Luiz (2008, p. 73), criticizes the term "relativization of res judicata". He argues that res judicata has never been absolute; in fact, it has always been relative. Suffice it to cite as examples the rescissory action in civil proceedings and the criminal review in criminal proceedings. In fact, what the authors want is to extend the limits of the relativization of res judicata.

The great controversy surrounding the relativization of res judicata concerns whether it can be applied to unjust judgments. Jose Delgado, a great defender of the relativization of res judicata, states that unjust judgments cannot become res judicata. After describing a list of situations considered unjust, he concludes that a judgment that is unjust can be overturned at any time, "because it is an attack on the democratic regime in its most consistent aspect, which is the guarantee of morality, legality, respect for the Constitution and the delivery of justice." (CORTES, 2008, p. 81).

Andre Luiz (2007, p. 74) and disagrees with the position of Justice Jose Delgado. In his words, *verbis*:

> What we cannot conceive of, however, is the intention to "relativize" res judicata, a procedural institute that guarantees legal certainty and, as such, an inseparable element of the Democratic Rule of Law, justifying such a proposal merely by invoking the occurrence of "injustice" in certain exceptional situations. The thesis is, with all *due* respect to those who defend it, untenable.

He concludes that relativizing res judicata based solely on the injustice of the decision could lead to a state of general insecurity. For him, the matter needs to be systematized, *verbis:*

> This is why many scholars point to the need to systematize the issue, including changing the legislation, so that the legal-procedural framework provides the doctrine of relativization with a sustainable basis for its safe application. (RAMOS, 2008, p. 79).

Brazilian jurisprudence has already accepted the thesis of relativization in some judgments. Some STJ Justices have expressed their positions, in their decisions, in the sense of superimposing other principles on the principle of legal certainty. Special Appeals numbered 226.436/PR are a case in point.
and 554.402/RS respectively:

> Res judicata, in the case of state actions, such as paternity investigation actions, must be interpreted *modus in rebus.* In the words of respectable and advanced doctrine, when scholars delve into the restudy of the institute, in the search above all for the realization of

due process, res judicata exists as a necessary creation for the practical security of legal relations and the difficulties that oppose its rupture are explained by the same reason. It must not be forgotten, however, that in a society of free men, justice must be above security, because without justice there is no freedom.
(...)
To the detriment of the public purse, it should not be allowed to cancel the incidence of double monetary correction, in disagreement with morality and the law. I repeat, both parties deserve ample protection, which is palpable in the protection of the principle of fair compensation.

Justice Salvio de Figueiredo, in REsp. 226.436/PR cited above, speaks of the overlapping of the value of justice over security. The case concerned a rescission action to carry out a DNA test that had not been carried out in the paternity investigation action. Critics of the relativization of res judicata understand that, in this case, the DNA test can be invoked as a new document, based on an extensive interpretation of article 485, item VII of the Code of Civil Procedure. The words of Barbosa Moreira, *apud* Andre Luiz (2008, p. 81), are precise:

It is worth noting that the Court *(referring to the STJ) in* no way declared the rescinded judgment "null and void", nor did it invent a new means of re-examining the matter. It merely brought the case within the scope of procedural law, through a perfectly reasonable relaxation of the concept of "new document". It managed to reconcile - and for this it deserves all praise - an alleged demand for justice with respect for the legal system.

The thesis of relativizing res judicata based on the injustice of judicial decisions cannot prosper, as it would create a situation of general insecurity. The injustices alleged by the plaintiffs as grounds for overturning res judicata can be included in the grounds for rescission under art. 485 of the CPC. The teachings of Andre Luiz (2008, p. 88) are conclusive:

The thesis of the "relativization" of res judicata based on the need to review *injustices*, therefore, does not seduce us, nor does it charm the majority of proceduralists. There are authors in the national doctrine who vehemently criticize it, as Nelson Nery Junior does. For this author, res judicata, due to its intrinsic relationship with the principle of legal certainty, is an element of the existence of the Democratic State of Law, and to preach its disregard in cases of alleged *injustice* is an idea of 'Nazi' origin.

These authors' criticisms are pertinent. But it cannot be denied that the relativization of res judicata has been gaining many supporters in the legal profession and that it will quickly be transformed into a rule by Brazilian legal practice. The doctrine needs to mature further in its studies on the subject and the legislature, the body responsible for creating procedural rules, needs to regulate the matter. Unconstitutional res judicata will be studied in the next section.

1.9 Unconstitutional res judicata in the context of the recent trend to relativize res judicata

After a brief analysis of the relativization of res judicata in Brazilian doctrine and jurisprudence, emphasizing the aspect of the injustice of decisions, it is up to us to make a more detailed study of this institute in the light of the control of constitutionality by the Federal Supreme Court.

The doctrinal current that defends the relativization of res judicata, led by Humberto Theodoro Junior (RAMOS, 2007, p. 92), argues that when the judgment contains unconstitutionality, it deserves different treatment from that given to illegal res judicata, because the taint of unconstitutionality is more serious.

The unconstitutional res judicata thesis, despite the criticisms of Marinoni (2008, p. 31) and Barbosa Moreira and Eduardo Talamini presented by Andre Luiz (2007, p. 92), has greater legal support than the unjust res judicata dealt with in the previous section. Case law and national legislation have given different treatment to this procedural phenomenon.

For a long time, the doctrine was that only legislative acts were subject to control. Andre Luiz (2007, p. 95) portrays this historical reality very well, after pointing out that the principle of constitutionality must be respected by all acts emanating from the government:

> This is important since, as Humberto Theodoro Junior observes - quoting Paulo Otero's liposophies - in the area of unconstitutionality, for a long time the attention and concern of jurists was focused on examining the constitutional non-conformity of legislative acts, which contributed to the institutionalization of the myth of the impermeability of res judicata court decisions, even if they contained defects of unconstitutionality.

Before the unconstitutional judgment becomes final, an extraordinary appeal to the Supreme Court (art. 102, III, 'a', CF/88) can be used as an instrument to correct the defect. If the interested party does not make use of the appeal to correct the defect, it will be left to file a rescission action (art. 485, V, of the CPC). Marinoni (2008, p.97) advises that unconstitutional judgments should be given more favorable treatment, such as not being subject to the two-year rescission period.

The rule in art. 485, V, speaks of violation of a literal provision of law. But the term "law" is interpreted extensively, in the sense that it also covers the Constitution. In this sense, Marinoni admits extensive interpretation, *verbis:*

The doctrine has extended the meaning of "literal violation of law", demonstrating that the very reason for rescission in the case of literal violation of infra-constitutional law could not exclude the admissibility of rescission in the case of literal violation of a constitutional rule.

When dealing with literal violation of the law, Sumula 343 of the Federal Supreme Court states that it is not possible to "bring an action for rescission for offense against a literal provision of law, when the rescinding decision was based on a legal text of controversial interpretation in the courts".

However, when the violation is of a constitutional rule that is controversial in the courts, this summary has no application. Both the Federal Supreme Court and the Superior Court of Justice have ruled along these lines, in line with the doctrine defending the relativization of unconstitutional res judicata. Justice Gilmar Mendes expressed this view in RE-ED 328812, published in the newspaper Diário de Justiga on 02.02.2008:

> It is based on the premise that a decision by the Federal Supreme Court is, in itself, sufficient proof of a literal violation of a constitutional rule. The basis of the rescission lies in the force of the Supreme Court's decision, regardless of the quality of the final decision, i.e. whether there was doubt in the courts about the (in)constitutionality of the rule or whether the interpretation directly violated the Constitution (MARINONI, 2008, P.99).

Marinoni (2008, p. 99) criticizes the idea that a rescission action is appropriate when the rescinded decision is based on a constitutional text whose interpretation is controversial in the courts. For him, it is inconceivable to attribute reasonable interpretations to infra-constitutional norms and a single possible interpretation to the constitutional norm, considering it to be of "correct interpretation". In his words (2008, p. 95-96), *verbis:*

> It is known, however, that the theory of "correct interpretation" has not been demonstrated to the satisfaction of the doctrine, just as there would be no reason to suppose that only a given quality of norm - the constitutional norm - could require a single interpretation. (...) To maintain the need for "correct" interpretation at the constitutional level and "reasonable" interpretation at the infra-constitutional level is an obvious *contradiction in terminis*, because the act of interpreting is one and the same when it comes to understanding legal norms.

The author's orientation is not widely accepted by the majority of legal scholars. The principle of the normative force of the Constitution and the maximum effectiveness of constitutional norms justifies the non-application of Summula 343 when the rescission action deals with constitutional matters. A brilliant passage by Andre Luiz (2007, p. 109) should be noted in this regard:

In our opinion, therefore, (i) the application of sumula no. 343 to so-called illegal res judicata is justified. 343 is justified for the so-called *illegal res judicata*, due to the need to give a restricted interpretation to the grounds for rescission and to pay homage to the principle of legal certainty represented by res judicata; and (ii) the non-application of the summary in question is also justified when there is a discussion of constitutional matters, this time in honor of the specific methods of constitutional interpretation and in obedience to the principles of the normative force of the Constitution and the maximum effectiveness of constitutional norms.

For Eduardo Talamini, apud Andre Luiz (2007, p. 110) it is not necessary for the interpretation to be divergent for the rescission action to be appropriate. It is enough that the interpretation is relevant. This is what the author says:

> (...) this exclusion (*from the application of STF summary n. 343*) is applicable to any case in which the constitutional question is involved, including when the rescinded judgment has unduly considered a rule to be unconstitutional (and this - it should be repeated - *regardless of* whether there is a manifestation of the Supreme Court, in a direct or incidental view, regarding the constitutionality of such a rule). In this case too, Sum. 343. Examining the compatibility of an infra-constitutional rule with the Constitution is obviously a constitutional matter. That is enough for Sum. 343 not to apply. (RAMOS, 2007, p. 110).

With regard to concentrated control, Article 27 of Law 9.688/99 allows the Supreme Court to give its decisions *ex nunc* effects. This article prescribes that for reasons of legal certainty or exceptional social interest, the STF may, by a majority of two thirds of its members, restrict the effects of the declaration of unconstitutionality or decide that it will only be effective from the date of final and unappealable decision or another moment that may be set. In this case, there is no need to discuss whether a rescission action can be brought on the grounds that the judgment is contrary to the STF's understanding.

The effects of the decision in diffuse control are controversial. The Federal Senate, when suspending a rule, does not usually state when its act will take effect. The recent understanding of doctrine and jurisprudence is that it is up to the STF, even in a specific case, to attribute one or other effect, especially when there is a need to limit the effects.

Marinoni's (2008, p. 105) criticisms regarding the rescission of sentences based on STF decisions in diffuse control are pertinent. For him, judges and courts, as well as the Supreme Court, when judging a specific case, are already carrying out diffuse control over the rules applied. He concludes that, *verbis:*

Instead of the retroactivity of the Supreme Court's decisions, it would be effectively and practically more convenient - obviously if this were legally possible and convenient in the Brazilian system (which it clearly isn't) - to remove the possibility of the ordinary judge controlling constitutionality (MARINONI, 2008, p. 105).

Finally, for those who argue that the unconstitutional judgment is non-existent, there is no need to even talk about relativizing res judicata. You can't relativize what doesn't exist. Therefore, they are not subject to the rescission period, because the defect is so serious that it prevents the formation of res judicata. In order to correct the defect, it would only be necessary to file a declaratory action. This is the main difference between non-existent judgments and null judgments. In the words of Jose Alexandre Manzano Oliani, *apud* Andre Luiz (2007, p. 137):

Relative nullities are remedied in the course of the proceedings and are subject to preclusion, with the result that they do not survive res judicata; absolute nullities survive res judicata and make the judgment rescindable, in other words, the null judgment becomes res judicata, but can be attacked by a rescission action; finally, legal non-existence is a defect of such intensity that the judgment affected by it does not become res judicata and is therefore open to attack by a declaratory action for the non-existence of a legal act, the filing of which is not subject to any kind of limitation period;
(...)
A final judgment based on a law that was later declared unconstitutional by the Supreme Court has concentrated control and is legally non-existent, above all because it applied a rule that does not exist in the respective legal system, in other words, it emerged from a process in which one of the conditions of the action was absent, namely: the legal possibility of the claim.

For the authors who defend the rescission of an unconstitutional judgment at any time, there is no practical difference between considering it null and non-existent. Humberto Theodoro, *apud* Andre Luiz (2008, p. 139), believes that unconstitutionality renders a judgment null and void and, as such, it can be argued and recognized at any time and in any process, by any judge or court. According to him, it is not possible to use a rescission action to set aside an unconstitutional judgment, as it is subject to a statute of limitations and is aimed at setting aside a valid judgment. An unconstitutional judgment is neither valid nor subject to a time limit.

For other authors, such as Francisco Barros Dias, Evandro Silva Barros and Ivo Dantas, cited by Andre Luiz (2007, p. 141-142), it is perfectly possible to use the rescission action, with no need to observe the statute of limitations when dealing with constitutional matters.

I disagree with all the differentiated treatment given by the aforementioned doctrine. The differentiated treatment given by the legal system to unconstitutional res judicata through the non-application of STF summa n. 343 to unconstitutional res judicata and the recent possibility of alleging the unenforceability of unconstitutional judgments (art. 741, paragraph and art. 475-L, paragraph 1, both of the CPC) is enough to favor constitutional norms. Therefore, the only differentiated treatment given to the rescission action, when it deals with a violation of a constitutional rule, is that it can be used even in cases where there is controversy in the case law of the lower courts.

Chapter 2: Binding precedents and precedents barring appeals

The reform of the judiciary, approved by Constitutional Amendment 45/2004, added article 103-A to the text of the Constitution, which deals with the Binding Summula. The sumula impeditiva de recurso was included in the same discussion, but was removed from the final text. The legislator regulated the institute in the Civil Procedure Code without giving it due attention, as will be seen below.

The binding summula aims to put an end to the resistance of lower courts to follow the guidelines already defined by higher courts. Osmar Mendes (200, p. 155), before Constitutional Amendment 45/2004, already criticized this, *verbis:*

> However, it is true that this is not always the case; on the contrary, there is sometimes a systematic resistance on the part of lower bodies, in the name of independence, to following the summaries and prevailing case law, which is a shame, as it goes against the principles of speed and effectiveness of judicial service.

The institute aims to combat this unfounded resistance, favoring the principle of equality of the parties in procedural relations. In order to understand its insertion into the Brazilian legal system, a study will be made of the behavior of judicial precedents in the common law and civil law legal systems.

2.1 The binding summa in the common law and civil law legal systems

Before delving into the study of binding precedents, it is important to understand the two legal systems and how jurisprudential precedents behave in relation to them.

The Common Law system developed in England from the 12th century through the decisions of the royal courts. It was also adopted by countries that modeled their law on English law, such as the United States.
According to Osmar Mendes (2008, p. 107), "this system is, from the outset, linked to royal power, and marked mainly by the appearance of the Royal Courts of Justice."

It was not up to the English parliament to create the rules to be applied by judges and courts. The rules were created by precedent. Osmar Mendes (2008, p. 111) is precise:

> And respect for previous case law, as well as precedents, demonstrates the greater concern

with resolving concrete cases effectively on a non-legislative basis. In fact, the system of precedents is a way of bringing legal certainty to an organization that does not have a strong written legislative basis.

Common law developed in opposition to the continental system of law, which was Roman by tradition and influenced by the barbarian peoples and canon law. Unlike the latter, English law is not a law of universities or principles, but a law of proceduralists and practitioners. Cassiano Luiz (2008, p. 55) accurately describes the birth of this law:

Around the 13th century, the decisions of magistrates began to circulate, and they were written down. Yearbooks were created which were the forerunners *of law reports,* repositories of judgments. The *common law* system thus developed in strict dependence on formalistic processes and, from a certain point onwards, began to find it difficult to develop and meet the needs of the time.

The precedents of English law arose from the lack of written legislation. Learning the law meant, in addition to learning the precedents, understanding the reasons behind the precedents. Deciding a case required determining which precedents were appropriate for the case in question. In the words of Osmar Mendes (2008, p. 112), *verbis:*

According to *Black's law dictionary, stare decisis* means "the doctrine of precedent, that a *court* must follow previous judicial decisions when the same points arise in new litigation". *Stare decisis* can also be referred to vertically or horizontally, depending on whether the lower courts are obliged to follow the precedents of the higher courts (of the same jurisdiction), or whether the courts follow their own precedents or those of a court of the same hierarchy.

It is worth noting that there was no legal rule imposing binding effect on precedent. However, judges often emphasized the importance of judgments as being the best interpreters of the law, and the requirement that such decisions should be followed in order to give certainty and continuity to the law. In the *common law* system, law is the fruit of experience. The judicial decision has the function of, in addition to settling the immediate controversy, establishing the precedent that will serve as a basis for future decisions, bringing legal certainty to the law.

The reliance on precedent developed in English law has also been adopted in the United States. The tradition of English law has not been transformed into a written rule and is not found in the English Constitution or laws. According to Osmar Mendes (2008, p. 114), the main objective of precedent is "to bring continuity, predictability, security and certainty to the system, as the primary source of *common law."* Although the United States has suffered a strong English influence, precedents are applied with greater flexibility, as it also uses written law to settle claims. Authors go so far as to say that American law is mixed. In the words of Decio Sebastiao (2006, p. 31):

> In the United States, unlike the English tradition, the Constitution is a normative document, a source of law, a written and consciously drafted norm, so the North American legal tradition is a process of rapprochement with the culture of Roman-German law, but in the meantime, precedents are also applied when settling disputes.

Even with the presence of legislated law, precedents have the same importance, or perhaps even a certain prevalence over the legislated norm, insofar as they explain what it definitely means.

It is worth mentioning Santor's link, in his work *Precedente Giudiziale, apud* Cassiano Luiz (2008, p. 64):

> Sartor apud CRUZ E TUCCI, op. cit., p. 179 et. seq., says that three effects can be granted to the decision that stops applying the precedent, setting a new paradigm:
> "a) *retrospective overruling,* when the overruling *has ex tunc* effect, not allowing the previous decision, which has now been replaced, to be invoked as a paradigm in previous cases awaiting judgment; b) *propspective overruling,* instituted by the American Supreme Court, in which the precedent is overruled with *ex nunc* effect, i.e. only in relation to successive cases, meaning that the *ratio decidendi* replaced continues to be emblematic, as a binding precedent, in relation to facts that have previously occurred; c) *anticipatory overruling*, introduced with unparalleled boldness by the United States Courts. It consists of the preventive overruling of a precedent by the lower courts, on the grounds that it no longer constitutes *good law,* as would have been recognized by the court *ad quem* itself.

The Brazilian Supreme Court's Sumula Vinculante is very similar to the American Supreme Court's *propspective overruling*[2] . Judicial decisions in the *Common Law* system are binding on future judges. They must be followed both by the issuing court (the Supreme Court) and by the lower courts. The case of Hutto v. Davis, translated by Osmar Mendes (2008, p. 132), expresses how the observance *of stare desisis* is obligatory*, verbis:*

> In the case of Hutto VS. Davis, of 1982, the Supreme Court called attention to the lower court *(Court of Appeal)* that did not follow a higher decision, stating that in doing so the *Court of Appeal* "consciously or unconsciously ignored the hierarchy of the federal court system created by the Constitution and Congress" and warned that "unless we wish anarchy to prevail over the federal judicial system, a precedent of this Court must be followed by the lower federal courts, regardless of what the judges of those courts think they are".

[2] This means that the new rule created by the judgment in the specific case only applies to future cases. The effects are ex nunc.

The Supreme Court has the task of interpreting the Constitution and creating precedents that become real constitutional norms.

From the 19th century onwards, some American states created a large number of laws on property, family law and inheritance, among others. These rules made the system of precedents more flexible, leading some authors to consider that the current American system is mixed.

With regard to the effects of precedents, Osmar Mendes concludes, translating the work of Zweigert and Kotz, that the American Court applies its precedents only to future cases, in the name of legal certainty. In his words (2008, p. 134):

> It is also interesting to note that, in the name of security, which is one of the objectives of the system of precedents, the doctrine and some US courts, in order to prevent the practice of *overruling a precedent* from bringing instability to social and economic relations, are adopting the system of *prospective overruling*, according to which the "new" rule created in a judgment (which represents a change in jurisprudence considering the precedents) will only be applied to future cases.

Another interesting point in English judicial precedents is the coexistence *of persuasive precedents* alongside *binding precedents.* These are binding on the other courts, like the recent Brazilian binding precedent. They can only cease to be applied if reviewed by the court or if the judge shows that there is a difference between the case to be decided and the precedent. *Persuasive precedents* only serve as arguments or grounds for the decision, without binding it. They are similar to the traditional summaries of the Brazilian Supreme Court and higher courts.

It is forgivable to recognize that, in recent times, English law is not only jurisprudential. The law legislated by parliament must be respected by the judge, unless it is reaffirmed by the courts. Osmar Mendes (2008) states that English *law* differs from the *law of civil law* countries. According to him, "English laws try to be as precise as possible, going down to the smallest detail even in the most trivial matters, adopting, more often than not, complex forms of expression." (CORTES, 2008, p. 123).

The emergence of written laws and the disappearance of the binding force of judicial precedents - with the exception of Supreme Court decisions, which continue to be binding - are proof of the approximation of the two systems: common law and civil law. Monica Sifuentes, *apud* Osmar Mendes (2008, p. 126), summarizes the matter well, *verbis*:

> The rapprochement between the two systems can be seen in the work of judges in written law countries, who, when faced with new situations that are not regulated by law, start to value the case-by-case nature of the problems being judged, to the detriment of a purely conceptual approach. The opposite is true of Anglo-American judges, who make increasing use of legal concepts as the basis for jurisprudential construction.

Having briefly considered judicial precedents in the common law system, it is now time to analyze how they behave in the Roman-Germanic system.

Roman law, the historical basis of Brazilian law, originated in the city of Rome in 754 BC. Throughout the Roman Empire, the law went through various phases until it reached the republican period, when the figure of the prudentes appeared, whose function was to fill in the gaps in the law.

The interpretation given by jurisprudents, according to Decio Sebastiao (2006, p. 27) is what is currently known as jurisprudence, i.e. the constant, uniform and harmonious succession of judgments handed down by the court in the same sense and direction and which crystallize in summaries. Jurisprudence at that time "was understood as the doctrine of jurisconsults, which in other words were 'opinions on existing opinions' that they issued." (DAIDONE, 2006, p. 29).

In the *civil law* system, the primary function of jurisprudence is to interpret the law. This is the primary source of the legal system used by the Romans to expand their empire over peoples of different traditions and cultures. Despite the fall of the Roman Empire, the legalistic tradition survived. In the words of Cassiano Luiz, *verbis:*

> The prevalence of law over any other source of law transcended the limits of the Roman Empire, whose fall did not prevent it from rising as the primary source of law. The growing influence of the Germanic peoples, in addition to reinforcing this trend, served as a prelude to the codification period of the 19th century.

Therefore, the distinction between *civil law* and *common law is* clear, because while the latter has an intense practice of stare decisis, the former is based on the premise that laws regulate social relations, and the role of judges is to apply and, at most, adapt abstract rules to specific cases. (CORTES, 2008)

In the 19th century, the countries of the Roman-German tradition, following the influence of the Code of Napoleon, published their codes and promulgated their constitutions, making them the basis of the entire legal system. In order to give meaning to the law and harmonize it with the political charter of the country, the courts came into being with the task of creating jurisprudence aimed at consolidating the interpretation of a given issue.

In principle, case law in Roman-Germanic countries is not binding. It only aims to serve as a foundation and example for future decisions, but does not necessarily oblige judges to follow it. It is forgiving to recognize that, even though it is not law, case law plays an important role in the constitution of law, because it is through interpretation that the general sense of the law is given guidance.

Osmar Mendes (2008, p. 154), expressing an opinion against recognizing case law as a formal source of law, states that:

> Admitting case law as a formal source of law, filling in gaps, goes against the system of the countries of the Roman-Germanic tradition, in which the judge has no creative role. They can even refer to and take as a basis some precedent, but it will always be based on the interpretation of some norm, be it a rule or a principle (positive or general law). (op. cit. p. 154).

Finally, the author concludes that, although it is not a formal source of law, the resistance of lower courts to follow the dominant summaries and jurisprudence of higher courts goes against the principles of speed and effectiveness of judicial service. In Brazil, Constitutional Amendment 45 of 2004 put an end to this disrespect and imposed the STF's consolidated decision, as will be studied in more detail in the next section.

2.2 The binding nature of judicial decisions in Brazilian law

The history of Brazilian law doesn't have much tradition with binding court decisions. The Civil Procedure Code of 1939 provided for the review appeal with the sole aim of standardizing case law. But the 1973 Code of Civil Procedure no longer dealt with it, and it only came into existence in the CLT, as an appellate instrument for the Superior Labor Court when the decision violates federal law, the Constitution or diverges from case law.

The Federal Supreme Court regulated the summary of dominant case law in 1963, giving it a merely persuasive character. The summary was regulated by Brazilian procedural legislation in 1973, in article 479 of the Code of Civil Procedure, which reads as follows: "A judgment taken by an absolute majority of the members of the court shall be the subject of a summary and shall constitute a precedent in the standardization of case law".

The Sumula provided for in the Code of Civil Procedure is merely persuasive. Referring to the Sumula, Justice Victor Nunes Leal, apud Cassiano Luiz (2008, p. 70), said that it represented a way of making the law more flexible. In his words, *verbis:*

> It stood between the implacable harshness of the old seats of the House of Suplicapao, for the general and perpetual intelligibility of the law, and the virtual inoperability of the prejulgados. It is a flexible instrument, which simplifies the work of justice at all levels, but avoids petrification, because the Sumula regulates the procedure by which it can be modified (...) It only requires, in order to be changed, more in-depth effort from lawyers and judges.
>
> They should look for new arguments, or unexplored aspects of old arguments, or highlight changes in social and economic reality. With this precaution, the summary replaces the judicial lottery of occasional majorities with the enlightened perseverance of genuine legal professionals.

When the 1973 Code was being drafted, the possibility of giving binding effect to court decisions was already being discussed. The conclusion of the committee reviewing the Code was that mandatory force, by procedural provision, violated the Federal Constitution.

The merely persuasive effect of the Sumula remained until December 31, 2004, when Constitutional Amendment no. 45 was enacted, adding art. 103 - A, with the following content:

> Art. 103-A. The Federal Supreme Court may, on its own initiative or on provocation, by decision of two thirds of its members, after repeated decisions on constitutional matters, approve a summary which, as from its publication in the official press, will have binding effect in relation to the other bodies of the Judiciary and the direct and indirect public administration, at federal, state and municipal level, as well as revise or cancel it, in the manner established by law.
>
> § Paragraph 1 - The purpose of the summary shall be to determine the validity, interpretation and efficacy of specific rules about which there is a current controversy between judicial bodies or between them and the public administration that causes serious legal uncertainty and a significant multiplication of cases on an identical issue.
>
> § Without prejudice to what may be established by law, the approval, revision or cancellation of a summary may be provoked by those who may bring a direct action for unconstitutionality.
>
> § Paragraph 3 - Any administrative act or judicial decision that contradicts the applicable summary or that unduly applies it shall be subject to a complaint to the Federal Supreme Court, which, if successful, shall annul the administrative act or set aside the judicial decision complained of, and order that another be issued with or without the application of the summary, as the case may be.

It is worth pointing out that the binding effect of judicial decisions in Brazil was nothing new with EC No. 45/2004. The Direct Action of Unconstitutionality and the Declaratory Action of Constitutionality (the latter inserted by Constitutional Amendment No. 3 of 1993) already provided for the binding effect of their decisions.

The fact is that the adoption of the Sumula Vinculante brings the *common law* and *civil law* systems closer together, to such an extent that the comparative study of the two has become a recurring theme in modern doctrine. Mancuso, *apud* Cassiano Luiz (2008, p. 76), supports the idea that the two systems are abandoning their purity and tending to form a mixed system. In his words:

> It doesn't seem far-fetched to conjecture that this gradual rapprochement between the two major legal regimes - that of the legal norm and that of judicial precedent - is in keeping with the contemporary context of a world society where interests, behaviors and needs increasingly communicate and interact, forming an immense *global village,* where old and entrenched legal differences between peoples, nations and states are fading (LURK, 2008, p. 76).

Integration between the two families is a notorious and irreversible fact in today's 21st century contemporary society. The master concludes:

> ...just another occurrence among the many globalizing events we are witnessing today, such as the issuance of a common currency (the euro) for the countries of continental Europe; understandings for the enactment of the same codified law for several countries, or even for an entire continent *(e.g.,* the so-called Standard Procedural Code for Latin America); the establishment of an economic and legal regime for countries that are geographically, economically and culturally close (*e.g.,* Mercosur); the establishment of international parameters for the reciprocal treatment of issues of common interest, such as the environment, immigration, compliance with judicial decisions; the repression of discriminatory practices; the preservation of human rights; the standardization of equipment, etc. (IURK, 2008, p. 77).

From the above, it can be seen that Brazil's adoption of the Sumula Vinculante comes as a natural process, with a view to giving the country's judiciary the necessary consistency and stability of judicial decisions. By binding judicial decisions, Brazil is bringing its reality into line with that of countries with continental law.

The *caput of* art. 103-A requires the fulfillment of two requirements for the issuance of a binding summary, namely the existence of repeated decisions on constitutional matters and a qualified quorum of two thirds or more of the members of the Court.

Another important point is that the binding nature of the rulings does not only apply to the judiciary, but also to direct and indirect administration at all levels. According to Osmar Mendes (2008, p. 193), by binding the administration, the summary runs the risk of violating the principle of the separation of powers enshrined in art. 2° of the Constitution of the Republic.

The above reasoning is coherent from a technical point of view, but in a practical sense, the extension of binding administrative decisions will represent a considerable procedural saving. When an administrative decision contravenes a binding precedent, it is not necessary for the injured party to take legal action to enforce their right. They can file a complaint directly with the Federal Supreme Court asking for the act contrary to the summa to be annulled.

2.3 The legal nature of binding sumulas

The great doctrinal debate concerns the behavior of the binding summa within the Brazilian legal system. For those who defend our law as being of Roman-Germanic tradition, the creation of general rules always falls to the legislature. The role of the judiciary is only interpretative and integrative.

In *common law* countries, *however*, as we have seen above, the judge has a creative role, as he often makes decisions without a legislative basis and these decisions become the basis for future ones.

Decio Sebastiao (2006, p. 47), in his comments on the legal nature of the institute, states that "by becoming part of our legal system, the binding summa, as is already the case in the Supreme Court, will also be a direct or immediate source of law and no longer indirect or optional". And he concludes that in view of its binding force, it is above case law, but below the legislated norm (law), since it does not derive from the bodies with constitutional competence to legislate. In this way, any supervening law that contradicts the summary has the power to remove its binding force. It will have to adapt to the new legal rules and in order to gain binding force it will have to go through a new and long jurisprudential process.

According to Jose Moura Rocha, quoted by Mancuso (DAIDONE, 2006, p. 48), "The summary is not simply the dominant or predominant case law. It is jurisprudence with an almost normative character...".

Part of the doctrine, such as Calmon de Passos, quoted by Decio Sebastiao (2006, p. 48), while recognizing that the sumula has only an interpretative function, equates it with the law because it is a general and abstract rule. In his words (2006, p. 48), *verbis:*

It remains to be seen what the consequences of this binding effect will be for the applicants and the judges. Consistent with our position, the summary, or case law with binding force, should be approximated to the general rule issued by the legislator. Neither can it be worth more, nor should it be worth less. Thus, its violation entails the same as any violation of the law by the magistrate, and it is not acceptable to give that violation privileged treatment."

Given that the binding summa originates from repeated decisions by the court in the same direction, when judging specific cases, it cannot attribute a normative character to the institute, since norms arise from general precepts intended to regulate social conduct. On the basis of these arguments, it can be affirmed that there is no usurpation of Congress' legislative competence in the issuance of case law summaries.

Recognizing the infra-legal nature of binding rulings, Osmar Mendes (2008, p. 197) states that "the legislator can change the content of a ruling issued by a court by issuing an express rule to the contrary". If the binding summary has the function of interpreting specific rules in which there is controversy, once the rule is revoked, the summary loses its purpose.

Decio Sebastiao (2006, p. 49) recognizes that there is a distinction between the binding summula and the law in its creation, but that the effects on third parties are similar.

In his words, *verbis*:

When drafting a legal rule, the legislator takes into account a combination of factors of socio-economic, political and cultural relevance, while the elements that form a binding summary will be the iterative and identical decisions on a given matter in the face of objective law. However, in practice, there is an approximation between the rule and the summary, because both must equally serve their recipients, who are the courts.

Even if it has a general nature, the summula cannot be given a normative nature, since its nature is that of an interpretative rule. For Osmar Mendes (2008, p. 199), "summaries are, in fact, the establishment of a certain interpretative meaning to a given rule, binding the factual hypothesis that gave rise to this interpretative meaning." Future decisions are bound by the interpretation given to the general rule (law) and not by the normative nature of the binding summary. And he concludes (2008, p. 200) that "the attribution of binding effect to the summary does not change its nature as a consolidated judicial decision based on the systematic repetition of an understanding in the same direction."

Therefore, although the binding summa is of a general nature and must be complied with by the bodies of the judiciary and direct and indirect public administration, it is not normative, but interpretative. To understand the institute differently would be to recognize its unconstitutionality as an offence to the constitutional principle of the separation of powers enshrined in Article 2 of the Constitution of the Republic.

2.4 The regulation of the binding summula by law n. 11.417/2006 and the RISTF.

Law 11.417, of December 20, 2006, which came into force on March 20, 2007, regulated article 103-A of the Federal Constitution, which deals with the creation, revision and cancellation of binding summaries.

Before going on to analyze the law, it should be noted that the procedure for issuing, revising and canceling binding precedents is not sufficiently disciplined. The law limits itself to establishing the qualified quorum for consideration by the plenary, the list of people entitled to bring a case with binding effect, the possibility of third parties expressing their opinion, the modulation of the material and temporal effects of the respective entry, the possibility of a complaint in the face of non-compliance with the binding summary, as well as the subsidiary application of the Internal Rules of the Federal Supreme Court.

As can be seen from the constitutional text and art. 2 of the regulatory law, the Supreme Court alone has the power to create binding summaries. In the text, the Superior Court of Justice was given the power to issue summaries, but when it was voted on in Congress, this text was removed.

Article 3 of the law broadened the list of those entitled to bring an action for the publication, revision and cancellation of a binding summary. To those already provided for in the constitutional text were added the General Public Defender of the Union; the Superior Courts, the Courts of Justice of the States or of the Federal District and Territories, the Federal Regional Courts, the Regional Labor Courts, the Electoral Regional Courts and the Military Courts.

According to Osmar Mendes (2008, p. 212): "This expansion is extremely positive and is not prohibited by the Federal Constitution, which only provides for the legitimacy of those authorized to bring a direct action of unconstitutionality, not establishing an exhaustive list in art. 103-A."

This increase contributes to reducing the risk of plastering over summarized case law.

The law did not actively legitimize the municipality to propose the publication, revision or cancellation of rulings, but it did provide, in §1 of art. 3, the possibility of formulating a proposal for a ruling, as long as it is made incidentally to the course of an action in which it is a party. In his comments on this paragraph, Osmar Mendes (2008, p. 213) comments on the importance of the incidental motion for a preliminary ruling, but regrets the fact that it is restricted to municipalities only. In his words:

> It seems to us that this possibility of an incidental plea is extremely important and deserves to be expressly extended to all legitimate parties. We disagree, however, with the restriction on the suspension of proceedings, which should occur under penalty of having, in a short space of time, a decision contrary to the binding summary. The legislator should have been more concerned about the possibility of decisions being taken contrary to the binding precedent, especially considering the narrow limit for reforming a decision after it has been taken in disagreement with the precedent (especially if it predates the edict).

The third-party manifestation is provided for in § 2 of art. 3 of law 11. 417/2006, similar to art. 7, § 2 of law 9868/1999, which deals with the direct action of unconstitutionality. It is worth noting that this is not a third-party intervention as provided for in the Code of Civil Procedure. In the latter, an interested third party is anyone who, even if they are not a party to the original legal relationship discussed in court, may be able to bear its economic or legal effects in the event of the enforcement of a judgment. Therefore, even if they have no direct link with the legitimate parties, the third party has a personal interest in the eventual outcome of the dispute, and is therefore only allowed to sue in subjective proceedings.

The words of Leonardo Vizeu Figueiredo[3] , in a text published on "the binding summula and law 11.417 of 2006", are precise:

> Since the procedure for issuing, revising or canceling a binding summa is an objective procedure of the Pretorio Excelso, the manifestation of third parties should only be limited to the exposition of a legal thesis on the validity, interpretation and effectiveness of the legal norms confronted with the constitutional text, the admission of which will depend on the prudent judgment of the rapporteur, and there is no need to speak of the defense of subjective interests.

The final part of the aforementioned paragraph gave the Supreme Court the power to regulate the participation of third parties. In compliance with the legal

[3] Text available at: http://jus2.uol.com.br/doutrina/texto.asp?id=9400. Accessed on: April 09, 2009.

mandate, Resolution 388, of December 5, 2008, provides in Article 3 that "The manifestation of any interested parties and the Attorney General of the Republic will take place in plenary session, when appropriate." From the above, it can be seen that the Supreme Court did not give due importance to the figure of the third-party manifestation, as it should have done.

Article 4 is of vital importance for studying the effects of binding precedents. The article states that:

> Art. 4 - A summary with binding effect shall have immediate effect, but the Federal Supreme Court, by decision of 2/3 (two thirds) of its members, may restrict the binding effects or decide that it shall only have effect from another time, in view of reasons of legal certainty or exceptional public interest.

Like Article 27 of the ADC and ADIn laws, the ordinary legislator has authorized the Supreme Court to restrict the effects of the summary or to apply them from another time. If the Supreme Court does not rule on the matter, it means that the effectiveness of the summary is immediate.

Article 5 stipulates that "if the law on which the binding summary was based is revoked or modified, the Federal Supreme Court, ex officio or upon provocation, shall review or cancel it, as the case may be". This article demonstrates that the legislature, when exercising its legislative activity, is not bound by the summary. It is also clear that the function of the summary is to interpret the norm (law), not to create it.

Article 7 repeats the rule laid down in the Federal Constitution, with a novelty in paragraph 1, in the sense that a complaint to the Federal Supreme Court is only admissible if administrative appeals have been exhausted.

Finally, art. 10 of the law establishes that the Supreme Court's internal rules may establish subsidiary rules on the procedure for issuing, revising or canceling binding rulings. So far, however, the Supreme Court has only issued two resolutions (Resolution No. 381 of October 29, 2008 and Resolution No. 388 of December 5, 2008) repeating what the Constitution and Law No. 11.417/2006 already provide, without introducing anything new. Many problems are bound to arise, especially with regard to revising and canceling summaries.

2.5 Res judicata and legal certainty in the face of binding effect

In recent decades, much has been discussed about the effectiveness of the fundamental rights enshrined in the Constitution. One of these rights that has aroused a lot of interest among scholars is the right to equality. In the beginning, the concern was limited to just guaranteeing rights, meaning mere formal equality of those subject to jurisdiction.

What we're looking for today is material equality. This aims to treat equals equally and unequals unequally. Aware of this reality, the legislator has created various laws to minimize the inequalities presented, such as the Statute for Children and Adolescents, the Consumer Protection Code and the Statute for the Elderly. All of these laws provided for mechanisms to defend unavailable individual and collective rights by means of extraordinary legitimates, such as trade associations, the public prosecutor's office and public administration entities and bodies.

However, legal mechanisms to protect equality are not enough to make the right effective. The judge state must respect equality. Cassiano Luiz (2008, p. 96) makes a precise point in this regard, *verbis:*

> The right to equality, therefore, cannot be thought of exclusively as a right to defense, since it must also consist of a service provided by the state.
> This means that if the legislature, when it enacts rules of substantive law and procedural law (because it must provide effective instruments of protection), must guarantee material equality, in the same way this guarantee must be ensured by the state-judge when he makes his decision. In this respect, we believe that the granting of the binding summary will bring the desired material equality to the courts, since despite its traditional formalization in the text of the Federal Constitution, there are still judicial decisions that violate the principle of equality, i.e. decisions that, even when dealing with identical issues, give the courts diametrically opposed answers, without any legitimate discriminatory criteria.

There would be no point in everyone being equal before the law if, before the courts, some are treated differently from others. The pursuit of equality for all before the State judge is a value sought by the principle of legal certainty.

The realization of the principle of equality sought by the binding summa, in the form advocated by the legislator, will have consequences for the res judicata that will be formed in matters still pending judgment. Cassiano Luiz (2008, p. 98-99) warns that even in the face of the existence of various defense mechanisms, it is common for res judicata to be formed with totally different results in substantially identical cases. This will be rejected:

> With the binding summary, and in pending and future concrete cases in which it is the basis for a decision, the parties will be treated by the state in an equal manner, i.e. beyond the legislated rule, they will effectively have equality observed in its application, which should be a guarantee for them (IURK, 2008, p. 98-99).

The effects of res judicata, defended by the Liebmanian doctrine, acquire new contours in the face of the binding summa. It is worth noting that it had already undergone major changes, when collective actions made it possible to subjectively extend the judgment to those who were not originally a party (erga omnes or ultra partes effect).

Even with the emergence of collective claims, several flaws were still present in the claims, leading to divergent results. In addition, the masses were not reached by collective actions. The binding summa emerges as yet another mechanism to expand judicial protection. In the precise words of Cassiano Luiz (2008, p. 109), *verbis:*

> In the same way that the traditional model proved insufficient, at a given historical moment, to provide adequate responses to the massification of social conflicts, giving rise to collective demands, the continuity of such failures led to the creation of mechanisms to expand judicial protection.
> The binding precedent, in this sense, brings the collective dimension closer to the individual dimension, influencing it, since it will bring to individual claims, in essence, a concern of a collective nature, subsisting in the standardization of the judicial response. In this sense, the individual is considered fundamentally as a component of a collective, and in both dimensions, the response to claims will be permeated by material equality.

The binding summa produces res judicata with effect for the future, i.e. at the time of filing the appeal, the party claims that the judge has to decide the case in the way provided for in the summa, because when the Supreme Court makes a summa, it becomes "res judicata" for future appeals.

The binding effect of the Supreme Court's decisions comes as an attempt to extend the limits of res judicata, since it binds the bodies and authorities that had not been part of the process, forcing them to adapt their future decisions to the guidance summarized by the Supreme Court.

It remains to be seen whether, once a summary has been issued with binding effect, it will have the power to affect res judicata that is contrary to the position of the Supreme Court. As seen in the previous chapter, the ordinary means of challenging a final judgment is the rescission action provided for in art.
485 of the CPC.

Doctrine differs as to whether rescission is appropriate when the STF decides against a final and unappealable judgment. Gilmar Ferreira Mendes, *apud* Cassiano Luiz (2008, p. 119) corroborates the idea of the non-retroactivity of the effects of the decision in the control of constitutionality:

> The Brazilian constitutionality control system seems to have an express exception to this strict doctrine of retroactivity: res judicata. Although the doctrine does not refer to this peculiarity, it is certain that the pronouncement of unconstitutionality does not make a mockery of res judicata, erected by the constitution as a constitutional guarantee (CF, art. 153, § 3). Even if it is not possible to consider an acquired right or a perfect juridical act based on an unconstitutional law, it is clear that the nullity *in tunc* does not affect the concrete rule contained in the sentence or judgment.

Despite the fact that the binding summa is different in nature from the direct action for constitutionality, the above arguments serve to establish a position in which it is impossible to grant *ex tunc* effects to the binding summa, since it should have no influence on final judgments that are based on an opinion contrary to the summa.

According to Cassiano (2008, p. 120), "the exceptions would be criminal norms, whose constitutional provision of more benign retroactivity (art. 5, XL) authorizes criminal review, and continuing legal relationships, which according to article 471 of the CPC...".

Despite having *erga omnes* effect and binding the other organs of the judiciary and the public administration, the binding summary is not the same as a law, and it is not possible to bring a rescission action on the basis of article 485, V of the Code of Civil Procedure (violation of a literal provision of law). To allow a judgment to be altered by a future interpretation by the Supreme Court would be to deny legal certainty and the stability of decisions, which is the aim of the binding precedent. In line with these arguments, Cassiano (2008, p. 122) concludes that "it is impossible for the binding summary to become an instrument justifying the relativization of res judicata, otherwise the institute will be completely emptied".

In the same vein is the content of the recent summa 743 of the Federal Supreme Court, according to which "a complaint cannot be lodged when the judicial act which is alleged to have contravened a decision of the Federal Supreme Court has already become final". Osmar Mendes (2008, p. 228-229) corroborates this view:

> Furthermore, the Supreme Court cannot become a forum for re-examining the conformity of

all judgments with binding sumulas, otherwise an institute that came to relieve the Court will become a source of countless new original actions (complaints).
The existence of a binding summa does not authorize the relativization of res judicata, which is very restricted, as already noted in a specific topic, limited to the legal hypotheses and the declaration of (in)constitutionality of the rule that served as the basis for the decision (and even then within a time limit).

It has been controversial whether res judicata was formed before the binding summa was issued, or before binding effects were given to the pre-existing summa. For the same reasons given above, legal certainty cannot be invoked as a basis for overturning res judicata. The consequences of revising or canceling res judicata will be studied in more detail in the next chapter.

2.6 Sumula impeditiva de recursos

Included in the reform package for the judiciary by the constituent legislator was the insertion in the constitutional text of the summary preventing appeals. The Senate's substitute to Constitutional Amendment Proposal no. 29/2000 made provision in our legal system for a summary with the effect of preventing appeals to the Federal Supreme Court and the Superior Labor Court, when the decision was handed down in accordance with the case law of the respective courts, by inserting article 105-A into the constitution, with the following wording:

Art. 105-A. The Superior Court of Justice may, of its own motion or on provocation, by decision of two thirds of its members, after repeated decisions on constitutional matters, approve a summary which, as from its publication, will constitute an impediment to the lodging of any appeals against a decision that has applied it, as well as review or cancel it, in the manner established by law.
§ Paragraph 1 - The purpose of the summary shall be to determine the validity, interpretation and efficacy of specific rules about which there is a current controversy between judicial bodies or between them and the public administration that causes serious legal uncertainty and a significant multiplication of cases on an identical issue.
§ Without prejudice to what may be established by law, the approval, revision or cancellation of a summary may be brought originally before the Superior Court of Justice by those who may bring a direct action for unconstitutionality.
§ Paragraph 3. Judicial decisions, at any level, that give a treaty or federal law the interpretation determined by the summary preventing appeal are not subject to appeal or any other means of challenge.

The text of art. 111-B of the Constitution was the same, as far as the Superior Labor Court was concerned.

Reading the normative text, one can see a strong approximation between the institutes of the binding summula and the sumula impeditiva de recurso. The brilliant words of Decio Sebastiao (2006, p. 83) in his comments on the proposal for constitutional amendment n. 29/2000 are *worth* noting:

> The "sumulas impeditivas" differ little from the "sumulas vinculantes" of the Federal Supreme Court in terms of their final effects within the process, since, as can be deduced from the names themselves, some "prevent" appeals against decisions made on the basis of the sumulas, while the others "bind" the judge himself, and therefore, at the outset, from making decisions that go against the sumulas.

The sumula impeditiva was criticized by most legal scholars on the grounds that to admit it would be to deny the constitutionally guaranteed double degree of jurisdiction. For the losing side, such as Miguel Reale Junior (DAIDONE, 2006, p. 84), the approval of the sumula impeditiva "would be the best solution to the Judiciary's procedural backlog and perhaps better than the binding sumular system, as it does not aggressively influence the magistrates' freedom of decision and the limits of access to the Supreme Courts".

In the same vein, Decio Sebastiao (2006, p. 87-88) expressed himself, *verbis*:

> The fact that the judge has to apply the law, be impartial in providing judicial services and have limited power to interpret what is laid down in the law, are necessary factors in order to provide legal certainty for him and his judgments. However, today we are faced with different and contradictory judgments, which leads us to believe that the binding or impeding summary is necessary to give harmony and equality to judicial decisions.
>
> Judges must have the freedom to interpret the law, but in the name of that freedom, they must not allow themselves to be influenced by their personal feelings and ideologies, but rather by their reason, albeit often instinctive, in other words, they must have a freedom restricted by majority jurisprudence that has already exhaustively interpreted the law, in order to guarantee their impersonality in the exercise of jurisdiction.

According to Calmon Passos, both types of summation (i.e. binding summation and summation preventing appeals) are consistent with the principle of legality, as they reinforce the interpretation of the legal text for identical cases, since they bind the judge and the parties, respectively, in the case of binding summation and summation preventing appeals.

It so happens that the sumula impeditiva of appeals was abandoned by the judicial reform, due to fierce criticism from opponents. At that time, Congress only managed to approve the binding precedent.

But the debate on the subject returned in 2006 with the reform of the Code of Civil Procedure. Paragraph 1 was inserted into article 518 of the CPC, with the following wording: "The judge shall not hear an appeal when the judgment is in accordance with a precedent of the Superior Court of Justice or the Federal Supreme Court".

In his favorable opinion, the rapporteur, Deputy Inaldo Leitao (NERY JUNIOR, 2007, p. 863), stated that:

> It is necessary to pay attention to the recent publication of the aforementioned Constitutional Amendment 45/2004 (Reform of the Judiciary), which adopted, within the scope of the Federal Supreme Court, the so-called binding summary, adding article 103-A to the Constitution of the Republic. (...) It should be noted, therefore, that the rejection of appeals against judgments that are in line with Supreme Court rulings is, in our opinion, a measure that is consistent with the adoption of the binding rulings.

The purpose of the appeal barring summary is to reduce the number of appeals that reach the courts, many of which have already been exhaustively debated and have been consolidated by the higher courts.

The scope of the sumula impeditiva is restricted to appeals. It does not have the breadth envisaged in the Constitutional Amendment bill rejected by Congress. Part of the doctrine criticizes the insertion of this institute by ordinary law, rejecting it as unconstitutional. Nelson Nery (2007, p. 863) speaks in this vein*:*

> CPC 518 § 1 is practically a copy of a provision that was not approved by EC 45/04 and there is a proposal in the National Congress to include the institute of the summula impeditiva de recurso in the text of the CF. the issue, therefore, is not one of ordinary law but of the Constitution. The provision means that, in practice, the simple summaries of the STF and the STJ all have binding effect, in clear disrespect for the constitutional system, especially the spirit of CF 103-A.

Nelson Nery's criticisms are only partly correct. If the appealing party does not agree with the judge's decision, they can file an interlocutory appeal with the court, which will be heard by the rapporteur. If the rapporteur decides that it is not appropriate, based on Article 557 of the Code of Civil Procedure, the non-compliant party can file an interlocutory appeal, under the terms of Paragraph 1 of the aforementioned article. Therefore, it is undeniable that the double degree of jurisdiction continues to be protected by the legal system.

The timidity of the legislator, in wanting to implement such a complex institute as the sumula impeditiva de recurso by inserting just one paragraph in the Code of Civil Procedure, renders the rule devoid of practical effects. It should have been included in the text of the Constitution and regulated by ordinary law, along the lines of the binding summary.

CHAPTER 3. THE CONSEQUENCES OF REVISING OR CANCELING THE BINDING SUMMARY FOR RES JUDICATA.

After studying the institute of res judicata and analyzing the binding summary in the light of the relativization of res judicata, it is important to observe the consequences caused by the revision or cancellation of the summarized understanding.

The process of reviewing and canceling binding precedents is a typical objective process, despite the fact that it establishes a consolidated understanding arising from a subjective process. But it differs from the process of abstract control of constitutionality in that the latter is based on the contrast, in theory, of the rules in conflict, and not on concrete cases.

There is a view against extending the relativization of res judicata to cases of revision or cancellation of binding precedents. Marinoni (2008, p. 86), a defender of res judicata, argues that a change in the court's understanding does not affect a final judgment. In his words (2008, p. 86), *verbis:* "a simple alteration in the normative or hermeneutic plan does not justify, in the face of invariable factual situations, the removal of the res judicata decision".

3.1 Similarities and differences between the binding summary and the ADI/ADC.

The binding summary is similar in many respects to the Direct Action of Unconstitutionality and the Declaratory Action of Constitutionality. As for the effects, during the processing of PEC 54/1995 in the National Congress, the possibility of equating them, as was done in relation to ADI and ADC, was discussed on many occasions. Along these lines was the proposal for amendment no. 2 of PEC no. 54/95 to § 2 of art. 102 of the Federal Constitution, authored by Senator Jose Serra, *verbis:*

> Art. 102...
> § Paragraph 2 - The Federal Supreme Court's final decisions on the merits of direct actions of constitutionality and unconstitutionality, as well as the summaries approved by an absolute majority of the Court, shall be published in the official gazette, shall be effective against all and shall have binding effects in relation to the other organs of the judiciary and the direct and indirect public administration of the Union, the States, the Federal District or the Municipalities.

This text underwent several modifications until the binding sumula was removed from the joint treatment and dealt with in a separate article. Following the coherence of the legislator, some comments will be made on the constitutional supports (direct action of unconstitutionality and declaratory action of constitutionality) and then the binding summary will be studied.

3.1.1 Direct action for unconstitutionality and declaratory action for constitutionality

The original constitution, concerned about the effectiveness of constitutional norms, created mechanisms to protect the constitution, through which it controls the acts of the secondary legislator. For control to exist, it is necessary to have a rigid constitution and a body with centralized competence, always responsible for the last word when the matter under discussion involves a constitutional norm.

In Brazil, the body responsible for the abstract control of the constitutionality of norms is the Supreme Court. But diffuse control can be exercised by any judge or court.

The object of concentrated control is the law or normative act in force which is incompatible with the constitution. Alexandre de Morais (2003, p. 607) believes that the control can only be carried out on norms in full force, since "there is no direct action for the unconstitutionality of a law or act that has already been repealed or whose effectiveness has already expired". Likewise, the appeal is dismissed:

> ... in the event that the contested law or normative act is repealed before the final judgment of the case, because, according to the Pretorio Excelso, the declaration in theory of a normative act that no longer exists, would transfer the direct action into a procedural instrument for the protection of personal and concrete legal situations. (MORALS, 2003, p. 607)

The word law is interpreted in a broad sense, encompassing all the normative species in art. 59 of the Federal Constitution, i.e. amendments to the Constitution, complementary laws, ordinary laws, delegated laws, provisional measures, legislative decrees and resolutions. Normative acts, on the other hand, do not have a well-defined delimitation. According to Pedro Lenza (2006, p.113), administrative acts, for control purposes, are the administrative decisions of judicial bodies, the resolutions of the International Labor Council, administrative resolutions, among others.

As for merely persuasive summaries, the Federal Supreme Court has already ruled, in ADIn 594-DF, that they cannot be challenged through concentrated control. Doubts have once again arisen about binding summaries, in the sense that they can be the subject of concentrated control. According to Pedro Lenza (2006, p. 114), sumulas are not subject to control by means of a direct action for unconstitutionality. In his words, *verbis:*

> Thus, in view of the fact that summaries are not marked by generality and abstraction, unlike laws, the technique of "constitutionality control" of summaries cannot be accepted, even in the case of binding summaries.
> What does exist is a review procedure through which the summary can be canceled. If it is canceled, this means that the previous position will no longer apply. In this case, of course, this new position will produce its consequences from the new understanding, binding the other organs of the judiciary and the direct and indirect public administration, at the federal, state and municipal levels.

The declaration of unconstitutionality of a law or normative act has retroactive and *erga omnes* effects, deconstructing the act declared unconstitutional from its origin, together with all the consequences derived from it, because unconstitutional acts are null and void, devoid of any legal efficacy. Even acts practiced on the basis of a rule declared unconstitutional are void.

However, by decision of two thirds of the members of the STF, the effects of the decision can be restricted, based on the rule contained in art. 27 of law n. 9868/1999. Gilmar Mendes *et al.* (2009, p. 1319), in their comments on the provision, point out that the limit is a consequence of the control itself and add that, *verbis*:

> The formula enshrined in the Portuguese Constitution and now partially reproduced in Article 27 of Law 9.868/99 is not an isolated model. On the contrary, it is a system that, positively or jurisprudentially, has been adopted by various systems of constitutionality control. In addition to the specific features of the German model, which have already been widely mentioned, it should be noted that the Austrian, Italian and Spanish systems and Community law itself have also adopted similar methods of restricting the effects of a declaration of nullity. American jurisprudence has also enshrined a mitigating model for absolute nullity.

As explained above, the principle of nullity is not absolute and is subject to restrictions, at the discretion of the Federal Supreme Court in the judgment of constitutional cases. It should be emphasized that nullity is the rule. The removal of nullity will depend on a severe weighing up which, based on the principle of proportionality, will allow the idea of legal certainty or another important constitutional principle to prevail, based on relevant social interest.

3.1.2 Binding summary.

The binding summula, in the same vein as the augurs studied above, aims to adapt the interpretation of norms to the Constitution. As the exercise of jurisdiction is open to several different bodies, it is natural for varying interpretations to emerge, not only of the meaning of constitutional precepts, but also of laws and normative acts in the light of the Constitution, leading to judicial discrepancies. The binding summa arises with the aim of standardizing the understanding of the Constitution, established by the constitutional jurisprudence of the Federal Supreme Court. In this situation, the Federal Supreme Court acts as the body that "closes" Brazil's constitutional jurisdiction, which means that the other courts must follow the constitutional interpretation consolidated by the Court's case law.

The legislator's concern in creating the binding summula was to promote legal certainty. In the words of Glauco Salomao (2007, p. 17), *verbis:*

> Therefore, compliance with the legal-constitutional interpretation established by the Federal Supreme Court in a binding summa acts to promote legal certainty and the isonomic application of the law, seeking to standardize constitutional exegesis. In short, it is an instrument that aims to prevent discriminatory treatment of equal situations in the application of the Constitution.

The great controversy over the institute under study concerns its suitability as diffuse or concentrated constitutional jurisdiction. As we saw at the beginning of this chapter, the discussions to equate it with ADI and ADC were so strong that the proposal for amendment no. 2 to PEC 54/95 regulated the effects of the three institutes in a single paragraph. But the legislator saw fit to separate the institutes in the final wording approved by Congress.

Glauco Salomao (2007, p. 18) believes that the binding summula has the nature of diffuse-concrete constitutional jurisdiction and concentrated-abstract jurisdiction. It is close to diffuse control, in that one of its presuppositions is the existence of a current disagreement on constitutional matters between judicial bodies or between them and the Public Administration. This disagreement stems from the various legal disputes brought before the country's courts and tribunals. In these legal disputes, in which the interpretation, validity or effectiveness of normative acts is discussed, it is common for different understandings to emerge about the same legal issue in the light of the Constitution. The Supreme Court, as guardian of the Constitution, will summarize the matter, putting an end to the disagreements, since its decision has binding effect and is effective against all.

The approximation to the abstract-concentrated model of constitutional jurisdiction is in terms of the binding nature of the decision against everyone. After commenting on the scope of the effects of the decision, Glauco Salomao (2007, p. 18) concludes that "the binding effect of the summaries is not substantially different from that of the decisions handed down in actions for the concentrated control of the constitutionality of laws and normative acts". Therefore, the decisions summarized by the STF, along with the direct action of unconstitutionality, declaratory action of constitutionality and argument of breach of fundamental precept, are endowed with binding effects. This is why the binding summa fits in part with the model of concentrated control in Brazil.

The scope of the binding summa concerns the validity, effectiveness and interpretation of certain rules dealing with constitutional matters, as provided for in §1 of art. 103-A of the FC. Neither the constitution nor the law has defined what validity, effectiveness and interpretation are. This task falls to the general theory of law, through doctrinal discussion. The majority of legal scholars have taken the view that the subject matter of a summary may be directly or indirectly related to the constitution. This is what Glauco Salomao (2007, p. 19) teaches, *verbis*:

> In this sense, the concepts of validity, interpretation and effectiveness, for the purposes of creating a binding summa, must have a direct connection with a given constitutional matter. It is believed, therefore, that controversies over infralegal acts and precepts in the face of the legal diploma on which they are based are excluded, since, in these situations, they only reflexively and indirectly affect constitutional material. Considering that the Federal Supreme Court, on several occasions, has stated that it does not admit extraordinary appeals when the alleged violation of the Constitution, if it existed, would only occur in a reflexive and indirect way, it would be incongruous to support the creation of binding summaries based on these controversies, if the very body competent to create them does not hear those disputes.

The word interpretation is a prior process of concluding on the validity and effectiveness of the rule that is the subject of the disagreement. In other words, it can only be said that a rule is constitutional or not after a prior process of interpretative activity. But there are those who believe that the insertion of this term serves to create a binding precedent when there are two or more equally valid interpretations of the same normative text in the face of the Constitution. Lenio Luis (2007, p. 165) puts *it* this way:

> [...] when the sole paragraph alludes to the expression 'interpretation of rules over which there is controversy', it certainly means legal provisions that have not been interpreted as unconstitutional (because if that were the case, the discussion would be restricted to their validity), but have been given different meanings by various courts, all of which, however, point to the non-validation of all or part of the provision.

Glauco Salomao (2007, p. 19) gives two examples of interpretative disagreements in constitutional matters that do not concern either the validity or the effectiveness of the rule. The first deals with the reception or non-reception of rules that predate the constitution. In this case, the phenomenon reaches the level of the existence of the rule. The validity or effectiveness of the rule is not discussed, as it was produced on the basis of the repealed constitutional rule. The second example cited by the author "concerns the interpretation of the original constitutional statements themselves, in which case there is no contrast between the infra-constitutional rules and the former". (2007, p. 19). In this case, the discussion revolves directly around the meaning and scope of the precepts of the Constitution as drawn up by the original constituent, without involving, as has been said, tho question of their validity, as it is unacceptable, or their effectiveness, as this is a different hypothesis.

On the basis of the above arguments, it can be seen that the constitution has given a great deal of leeway to the creation of binding summaries, going beyond the limits imposed on the declaratory action of constitutionality.

One point that has been highlighted is when the binding summary declares the unconstitutionality of a rule on the basis of repeated decisions in an extraordinary appeal. Part of the doctrine argues that, for the rule to produce *erga omnes* effects, it must be submitted to the Senate, based on art. 52, X of the Federal Constitution. This orientation should not be followed, because if the legislator had intended to submit the rule to the Senate for consideration, he would have done so, as he did in relation to diffuse control. In this sense, Glauco Salomao (2007, p. 21) advises, *verbis*:

> ... it is well known that declarations of unconstitutionality in abstract control lead to the exclusion of the rule from the system, in other words, the illegitimate act is nullified definitively. The same would happen with binding summaries, since, although they were born in the diffuse-concrete system, they enter the abstract-concentrated system by virtue of their binding effect. From this perspective, when the Federal Supreme Court issues a binding

summa pronouncing the unconstitutionality of a certain rule, that rule will be annulled and cease to exist legally.

Therefore, the senate's power to grant binding effect to Supreme Court decisions is restricted to cases of mere declarations of unconstitutionality in the diffuse control of constitutionality. If, by any chance, the Supreme Court decides to give binding effect to its decision, the Senate's review is prejudiced by an express constitutional imperative. Proposed amendment no. 7 to PEC 54/95 was worded in such a way as to give binding effect to the summula only if approved by a Senate resolution. However, this text was not approved, and was worded as follows, *verbis:* "XI - to attribute to the final decisions on the merits, handed down by the Federal Supreme Court, after they have been summarized, efficacy against all and binding effect, in relation to the other bodies of the Judiciary and the Executive Branch". (BRASIL, 1999, p. 62).

Finally, there are those who argue that art. 52, X of the FC would be repealed by constitutional change, such as Gilmar Mendes (2008, p. 270-280), in his book "Fundamental Rights and Constitutionality Control". Even in diffuse control, the Supreme Court's decisions would have effects against everyone. In the same vein, the aforementioned author expressed himself in the question of order in the judgment of RCL n. 4.335/AC, of which he is rapporteur, according to STF informative n. 463. The arguments are not convincing, because if the Supreme Court wants to give its decisions in diffuse control a general character, without the intervention of the Senate, it should issue a binding summary.

The binding summary has a broader scope than the constitutional augurs of concentrated control. It differs from these institutes in terms of the process that gives rise to the summula, since the former is developed through an objective process, while the latter originates from repeated court decisions. In other respects, the sumula is similar to abstract constitutionality actions, as can be seen in the comparative reading of the topics above.

3.2 Violation of res judicata as an instrument of rescission.

With an apparently contradictory text, item IV provides for rescission in the event of a breach of res judicata. I say contradictory because in all the sections of the aforementioned article, the court decision that can be rescinded has already become final.

Material res judicata, as seen above, is the quality of a judgment that makes it immutable and indisputable, no longer subject to ordinary or extraordinary appeal. For Nelson Nery (2007, p. 680), "legal certainty, brought about by res judicata, is a manifestation of the Democratic Rule of Law".

A judgment that offends res judicata, for critics of the relativization of res judicata, is considered non-existent and has no effect whatsoever. Nelson Nery (2007, p. 779), commenting on Alvim Wambier's view, states that it is unnecessary to file a rescission action to set aside a judgment that has been rendered in breach of res judicata, because:

> As there is no judgment, res judicata has not been formed, so that, for this trend, the discussion about which res judicata prevails, whether the first or the second, is a false problem: the issue is resolved by the assertion that there was only one - the first - res judicata. Since it is unnecessary to overturn the second res judicata, because it has not been formed, it is enough for the party or interested party to allege this non-existence in ongoing proceedings, or to file an action for a declaration of non-existence. In the case of the non-existence of a judgment and res judicata, there is no time limit for this allegation (at any time and at any level of jurisdiction), nor for exercising the negative declaratory action (perpetual claim).

In the case of an action for rescission based on res judicata, once the party's claim has been upheld, the court does not proceed to a new trial. In the other cases of art. 485 of the CPC, as a rule, once the rescinding court has been upheld, it moves on to the rescinding court, i.e., it proceeds to a new trial. In the words of Osmar Mendes (2008, p. 67), *verbis:*

> In some cases, it may be that the rescission of the judgment alone exhausts the jurisdictional activity, as in the case of the rescission action being accepted and upheld for an offense against res judicata - there will already be a previous decision that will be valid and take effect, and there will be no need to rejudge the matter.

On the basis of the arguments set out above, it is understood that it is not possible to use a rescission action to set aside a final judgment that contradicts the understanding embodied in a binding summary. If the review is carried out by means of a rescission, the judgment will not be valid because it offends res judicata. This is what Osmar Mendes (2008, p. 236) concludes, *verbis*:

> As explained above, an important value of the legal system that must be preserved is legal certainty, which is embodied in res judicata. It is true that the binding summary also aims to

ensure security, but respect for res judicata is fundamental to maintaining social order and respect for decisions and the judiciary itself.

Therefore, the rescission action is a procedural institute made available to the parties to invalidate a subsequent judgment handed down after a previous judgment has become final, as provided for in Article 485, IV of the Code of Civil Procedure. The exceptions are the other clauses of this article.

The examples given by the doctrine defending the rescission action against a judgment that disrespects the binding precedent are already protected because they fall under one of the clauses of article 485 of the CPC. For example, a judgment that goes against a precedent and invalidates an article of law on the grounds that it is unconstitutional can be rescinded, not because it violates the precedent, but because it is based on a law declared unconstitutional by the Supreme Court. Upholding such a decision contrary to constitutional interpretation goes against the normative force of the constitution and the principle of maximum effectiveness of the constitutional norm. That is why it must be rescinded, even if it is a summary of merely persuasive effect. The same reasoning applies when the judgment violates the interpretative summary of a law. The decision will be rescinded for violating an express provision of the law interpreted by the Supreme Court, but not for violating the binding summary. It is worth noting that the latter is not normative, but interpretative in the broad sense (interpretation, validity and effectiveness of specific rules).

3.3 The procedure for revising or canceling binding precedents

The process of revising and canceling binding precedents is much more difficult from a practical point of view than the process of creating them. To create a binding precedent, the succession of decisions in the same direction is used as the basis. In order to revise or cancel it, it is difficult to see repeated decisions that go against the binding summa, since it is fearful that the Supreme Court will rule against the summa. But that doesn't mean it's impossible, because the summary is not binding on the Court itself. It binds the other organs of the judiciary and the direct and indirect public administration.

It is worth noting that the legal system for creating, revising and canceling binding rulings is similar to an objective process, albeit with some nuances. Firstly, because this process does not discuss the subjective interests of individuals. These have already been assessed in concrete cases (subjective process), which have served as the basis for the formation of the Supreme Court's constitutional jurisprudence, in which the parties have even exercised their right to a fair hearing and a full defense. The deliberations on the summaries take place after the individual disputes have been resolved.

Glauco Salomao (2007, p. 37) and Andre Ramos (2006, p. 30) corroborate the view that the binding summa process is objective in nature. The rationale is that the legitimate parties do not act in pursuit of subjective and particular interests, although they may be moved by the institutional interests they represent. The lawsuit only aims to discuss the propriety of the legal-constitutional interpretation given by the court in the judgment of concrete cases. In this sense, Glauco Salomao (2007, p. 37), *verbis:*

> In view of the above, we can see that the legal system for creating, revising and canceling binding precedents is structured as an objective process. (...) The discussion surrounding the precedent is restricted to assessing whether a specific legal orientation established in the court's jurisprudence has binding force, or whether it is advisable to revise or cancel a previously existing precedent. Therefore, it is not used as an instrument for reviewing previous individual cases that have already been decided.

The binding nature of judicial decisions should not give rise to concern, as there is no danger that case law on the interpretation of the law will stagnate, since the courts are free to revise the summarized understanding. Decio Sebastiao (2006, p. 91) defends the flexible nature of the binding summa, *verbis*:

> As a procedural means of avoiding conflicting decisions on matters that have been exhaustively examined by the lower courts and especially by the higher courts, and which concern the dynamic society itself, as we have seen, the binding or impeding summary must have a flexible character that allows it to be revised or canceled.

On the other hand, the defenders of the summary reject the criticism that the case law is rigid. Even the law is subject to revision, repeal or derogation. For the same reason, binding rulings can be revised or canceled, as expressly provided for in Article 103-A of the Federal Constitution. It is up to lawyers and judges, when they consider that the summary has been exceeded, to "present new arguments and aspects that have not been explored in previous cases, as well as highlighting the changes that have occurred in the socio-economic context of the country".

(DAIDONE, 2006, p. 92).

In opposition to those who claim that law is petrified by the application of the summula, Decio Sebastiao (2006, p. 92) concludes that, *verbis*:

> From the above reading, one can conclude that the mandatory application of summaries does not mean that the decisions will have an eternal or petrified character, precisely because the aforementioned article 102-A of the Magna Carta expressly establishes the existence of flexibility in the form of revision or even cancellation of the entry.

According to the above arguments, it can be said that the summa represents the maturity of the courts' understanding of a particular issue.

controversial issue. However, this does not mean that the interpreters of the rule should not be attentive to social transformations. It is clear that revision or cancellation must go through a careful process, so that the theses arising from contrary decisions are observed, after repeated judgments, thus allowing jurisprudential mobility and also so that the desired security is not compromised.

Osmar Mendes (2008, p. 206), in his comments on the revision and cancellation of the binding summula, states that:

> It is essential that summaries are not issued and then revised or canceled, which would run counter to legal certainty. It should be repeated that one of the intentions of summaries is to give predictability to judicial decisions. Any issuance followed by successive revisions and/or cancellations shows, on the contrary, instability in the Court's jurisprudence, which is reflected in the unpredictability of decisions and runs counter to the function of summarized jurisprudence - to provide, on the basis of predictability, legal certainty.

Therefore, revision or cancellation should only take place when there is a real need due to new arguments and new aspects of the problem. In order to change your understanding, you must follow the previously established procedure, as explained below.

Those entitled to bring an action to revise or cancel a binding summa are the same as those entitled to bring an action to create one, i.e. the President of the Republic, the Board of the Federal Senate, the Board of the Chamber of Deputies, the Board of the Legislative Assembly or the Legislative Chamber of the Federal District, the Governor of a State or the Federal District, the Attorney General of the Republic, the Federal Council of the Brazilian Bar Association, a political party with representation in the National Congress, a trade union confederation or a nationwide class entity. In addition to the legal entities provided for in §2 of art. 103-A of the Constitution, law 11.4172006 extended jurisdiction to the Public Defender of the Union, the Supreme Courts, the Courts of Justice of the States or of the Federal District and Territories, the Federal Regional Courts, the Regional Labor Courts, the Regional Electoral Courts and the Military Courts. Finally, the Federal Supreme Court can also propose the revision or cancellation of its own motion, according to the combined interpretation of the head of art. 103-A and its paragraph 2.

The caput of art. 103-A stipulates that the same quorum is required for the approval of a binding summary, namely two thirds of the members of the STF. Repeating the Constitutional rule, §3 of art. 2 of law 11.417/2006 emphasized the need for a qualified quorum in a clearer way, *verbis:*"The approval, revision and cancellation of a summary with binding effect will depend on a decision taken by 2/3 (two thirds) of the Federal Supreme Court, in plenary session."

The controversial issue regarding the revision or cancellation of the summula concerns the need to issue repeated decisions, as a necessary condition for the procedure, just as it requires for the edipao. According to Andre Ramos (2006, p. 33), these decisions judged by the Supreme Court must be in the opposite direction to the summary, because if they are in the same direction, there is no point in revising or canceling them.

Glauco Salomao (2007, p. 45) does not corroborate the arguments of the above-mentioned author:

> (...) in order for a binding summula to have been created, it was necessary to construct a firm understanding of the Federal Supreme Court on constitutional matters. This summula reflects the legal-constitutional interpretation established by the highest body of Brazilian constitutional jurisdiction. In this sense, if the Federal Supreme Court begins to issue decisions that are at odds with a summary in force, the message transmitted to the other courts and the Public Administration is that it does not even recognize the constitutional jurisprudence previously developed as adequate. Thus, the Federal Supreme Court itself would be, albeit implicitly, authorizing other bodies to disapply a binding precedent it has produced. In this case, one would have to wonder about the very usefulness of a binding summa if the very body that drafts it could, at any time and in any way it pleases, decide otherwise.

The most coherent solution will be to suspend cases that discuss consistent arguments capable of changing the jurisprudence established in a binding summary, while debating the possibility of revising or canceling it. After deliberation, the Supreme Court will decide the case according to the new guidance. In this way, in addition to preserving the current interpretation, the Supreme Court changes its understanding without disrespecting the binding precedent in the application of the specific case.

However, Article 6 of Law 11.417/2006 states the opposite, as it prohibits the suspension of proceedings when discussing the revision or cancellation of a summary, *verbis:* "the proposal to issue, revise or cancel a binding summary does not authorize the suspension of proceedings in which the same issue is being discussed". The best doctrine believes that the legislator failed to apply the same rules for the issue of a summary to its revision or cancellation.

The importance of the sumula lies in the fact that it ensures the dynamism of the Supreme Court's jurisprudence without damaging legal certainty. As Candido Dinamarco, *apud* Glauco Salomao (2007, p. 46), observes:

> The noblest attribute of what is known as jurisprudential law is its ability to adapt to the nation's social and economic changes, in order to extract from constitutional and legal texts the norm that meets society's axiological values.

Another important fact in the process of reviewing and canceling binding precedents is the possibility of third parties expressing their opinion, at the discretion of the rapporteur, as provided for in art. 3, § 2 of law 11.417/2006. This third party is not the same as the interested third party provided for in the CPC. It is more akin to the *amicus ciriae,* present in the process of abstract control of norms (art. 7, § 2, of Law n. 9.868/99).

Finally, it is worth highlighting the need for the Attorney General of the Republic to express his opinion in cases in which he has not exercised active legitimacy, as provided for in paragraph 2 of art. 2 of the law under study, *verbis*: "Paragraph 2 The Attorney General of the Republic, in proposals that he has not formulated, shall express his opinion prior to the issuance, revision or cancellation of a binding precedent". In this case, he will not be acting as a party to the proceedings, but as a *custos legis.*

3.4 The effects of revising or canceling a binding summary on formal and material res judicata.

Having studied the institutes of res judicata and binding precedents, it remains to discuss the effects of canceling or revising them in the light of the modern trend towards relativizing res judicata. To this end, we will start with the following questions: Once it has been canceled or revised, will it be retroactive in order to affect consolidated situations? Does the binding summa constitute another hypothesis of relativization of res judicata?

In order to answer these questions, in the case of summaries dealing with constitutional matters, we will use as a basis the arguments produced in relation to the effectiveness of *erga omnes* declarations of constitutionality or unconstitutionality made by the Federal Supreme Court, in the context of concentrated control of norms. As for the summaries dealing with infra-constitutional matters, their effects will be studied in the light of summary 343 of the Federal Supreme Court.

Before going on to study the consequences of revising or canceling a binding summa for res judicata, some considerations will be made about tho emergence of the binding effect and *erga omnes* effectiveness in Brazilian law.

The institute of binding effect was introduced in Brazil in 1993 by Constitutional Amendment No. 3, inserting another form of abstract control of norms (declaratory action of constitutionality). Law 9868/99 extended these effects to direct actions of unconstitutionality.

The *erga omnes* effect does not affect the legislature in the exercise of its typical activity. Thus, the declaration of unconstitutionality of one rule does not invalidate the others, even if they have the same content. In this sense:

> However, erga omnes effectiveness, like res judicata, is restricted only to the operative part of the decision that recognizes the constitutionality or unconstitutionality of a rule. Thus, once a legal precept has been declared invalid, the decision only affects that precept and does not affect other acts with a similar content to the one considered illegitimate (LEITE, 2007, p. 51).

The binding effect means that the decision is binding beyond the particular case in which it is handed down. Glauco Salomao (2007, p. 51) summarizes the consequences of this effect well, *verbis:*

> From this it follows: (a) that these recipients, including those who did not take part in the

process, must adapt their conduct to the orientation set out in the ratio decidendi of the binding decision; (b) that acts with the same content as the one deemed unconstitutional must be annulled; (c) and that these recipients cannot adopt an interpretation that differs from the one accepted by the Court. In short, it could be said that the binding effect requires its recipients to take all possible steps to comply with the guidance set by the Court.

The binding effect and erga omnes efficacy of binding summa jurisprudence are not very different from those set out above for constitutional aegis of concentrated control. It has some peculiarities depending on the nature of the rule that the Supreme Court has summarized, as will be seen below.

The effects of binding rulings, in the subjective sphere, do not affect the Supreme Court, because if they did, it would be denying it the possibility of revising or canceling existing rulings. In the same way, the legislative power is not subject to the effects of a summary. Thus, from a legal point of view, there is nothing to prevent the legislature from contradicting a consolidated understanding in a binding precedent by means of a new legislative instrument. This was the orientation followed by the legislator in Article 5 of Law 11.417/2006, *verbis:* "Art. 5 - If the law on which the binding precedent was based is repealed or modified, the Federal Supreme Court, ex officio or on provocation, shall review or cancel it, as the case may be". However, if the ruling declares a law unconstitutional, even if the legislator creates another law along the same lines, it will not be able to take effect in the legal world, because the declaration of unconstitutionality on the previous law cannot be disregarded by a subsequent law. Art. 5 must be read as a summary that interprets the law without declaring it unconstitutional.

3.4.1 Binding rulings on constitutional matters

First of all, it should be pointed out that this issue is highly controversial in Brazilian doctrine. Various currents have emerged with the aim of defining the legal nature of the institute and delimiting its effects. When it comes to applying the effects, several doctrinal clashes arise due to conflicts of principles, such as the principle of legal certainty expressed in res judicata and the principle of equality.

The first binding rulings have behaved in various ways, sometimes exercising abstract control of norms (declaring the constitutionality or unconstitutionality of a law or normative act), sometimes interpreting the law and sometimes creating rules not provided for in the legal system.

When a summary declares a law unconstitutional, the same rules apply to its effects as for constitutional augurs. Therefore, as a rule, it has *ex tunc* effects, undoing all acts carried out under the aegis of the unconstitutional law, since it has been declared null and void and has no effect in the legal world. Res judicata is relativized in accordance with the principles of the normative force of the Constitution and the maximum effectiveness of constitutional norms, and rescission action can be used to overturn a final judgment.

Glauco Salomao (2007, p. 57) contests the attribution of *ex tunc* effects even if the ruling deals with constitutional matters. In his words:

> Once a binding summula has been approved, it will, as a rule, take effect "as from its publication in the official press" (art. 103-A, caput of the Federal Constitution). This means that binding rulings do not have retroactive effect (ex tunc), but only prospective effect (ex nunc), even in cases where they declare a certain rule unconstitutional. A relevant practical consequence of the binding summary's prospective effectiveness is that acts carried out before its publication in the official press are not affected by it. In fact, if the summary does not have retroactive effect, then all acts and business carried out prior to its publication will be preserved, even if they were carried out on the basis of a legal interpretation not accepted in the summary. Therefore, as a rule, a summary is only binding once it has been published.

The above arguments are not consistent with the hypothesis of creating a binding summary. It is appropriate to revise or cancel it, because in this case it cannot be given *ex tunc* effect, since the aim of revising or canceling the binding summary cannot offend the principle of legal certainty. Decisions taken on the basis of the previous binding summary must prevail, since there was no controversy over the rights of the parties at the time of the decision. In the case of the creation of a summary, the situation is completely different, since one of the requirements for the creation of a summary is that there be controversy in the decisions of the courts. The example cited by Andre Luiz (2007. P. 104) in his criticism of the relativization of res judicata in cases where the position of the Federal Supreme Court changes, *verbis:*

> Consider, for example, the following case: a certain decision becomes final and has adopted the prevailing position on the subject under discussion. One year after the decision has become final and unappealable - within the time limit for filing a rescission action - the case law on the subject changes. The rescission action is then filed, and the rescinded decision is reformed. However, as this is a controversial matter, it may be that, in the future, the jurisprudential understanding on the subject will change again, and the old position, the one adopted in the first decision, will prevail.

To rescind a judgment every time the Supreme Court changes its position would create chaos in the Brazilian legal system. It would generate a multiplication of lawsuits every time the Supreme Court changed its position, which would run counter to the principles that motivated the creation of the binding summary, which are legal certainty and the stability of decisions. Cassiano Luiz (2008, p. 120) has spoken out in this regard, *verbis*:

> In the same way, once the summary is canceled or revised, its effects should only be *ex nunc*, under penalty of subversion of the protection of legal certainty, and consequently, of the complex emptying of the institute of res judicata. Both the binding summary and the res judicata previously established are acts of the State-Judge that concern the moment of the decision, and so should only regulate future legal relations.
> The exceptions would be criminal rules, whose constitutional provision of more benign retroactivity (art. 5, XL) authorizes criminal review, and continuing legal relationships, which according to article 471 of the CPC give rise to review by changing the state of fact or law.

The interpretation of the institute in the light of the Federal Constitution leads to the conclusion that the effects of the binding summary are *erga omnes* and *ex nunc*. This was the intention of the derived constituent legislator in prescribing that "from its publication in the official press, it shall have binding effect in relation to the other organs of the Judiciary and the direct and indirect public administration, at federal, state and municipal level". Consistent with the grounds presented is the content of the recent summary n. 734 of the Federal Supreme Court, *verbis:* "No complaint may be lodged when the judicial act alleged to have contravened a decision of the Federal Supreme Court has already become final".

A situation that generates different effects is when the summary interprets a constitutional rule. According to Glauco Salomao (2007, p. 55), once the Supreme Court has interpreted a constitutional rule, the interpretation given by the ordinary legislator does not have the power to generate the revision or cancellation of the summary, based on art. 5 of law 11.417/2006.

It would only be revised or canceled if the change was made through a Constitutional Amendment. In this sense are his conclusions (2007, p. 55), *verbis*:

> As for the legislative instrument, it is believed that any binding summa resulting from a direct interpretation of constitutional statements would only be jeopardized if these statements were altered by a constitutional amendment. In fact, legally speaking, there is no other solution, since the constitutional text could not be altered by a legislative instrument that is hierarchically inferior to it. Thus, by giving a new treatment to a legal issue previously decided by the Supreme Court and consolidated in a binding summary, the newly-created amendment reopens the discussion, introducing elements that did not exist until then. The Court will have

to decide concrete cases based on the new legal discipline, while maintaining the precedent for situations that occurred before the amendment.

However, if the summula interprets a constitutional rule embodied in a petrea clause, not even a constitutional amendment has the power to cause the binding summula to be revised or canceled, since such rules are not subject to change.

3.4.2 Binding rulings on infra-constitutional matters

The wording of a binding summary ruling on the validity, interpretation or effectiveness of an infra-constitutional rule can be revised or canceled due to new guidance from the court or due to the rule being revoked by the legislative power.

Rescission proceedings are not appropriate to annul a judgment based on a law whose interpretation is controversial in the courts. This is the content of Summula 343 of the Federal Supreme Court, *verbis:* "a rescissionary appeal for infringement of a literal provision of law is not possible when the rescinded decision is based on a legal text whose interpretation is controversial in the courts".

According to the above statement, even if a new understanding is established after the decision has become final and unappealable, contrary to the one adopted by the judgment, the rescission action would be inapplicable. A judgment based on a binding precedent that is later canceled or revised cannot be rescinded, because at the time it was applied there was no controversy on the subject. On the contrary, the judge was obliged to apply the summary, under penalty of having his decision overturned by the Federal Supreme Court. The conclusions of Andre Luiz (2007, p. 104) in his comments on STF sumula n. 343 are precise, *verbis:*

> Now, it should not be forgotten that the right to bring an action for rescission is an extremely exceptional situation, insofar as it constitutes a concession made by the courts in order to seek *justice for decisions.* It cannot be understood, therefore, that a decision that reasonably applied the law, according to the majority view at a given time, should be considered offensive to the legal system simply because case law has changed, consolidating itself in the opposite direction. This is, in our humble opinion, the purpose of STF summa n. 343.

Sumula n. 343 of the STF, therefore, privileges legal certainty, recognizing as legitimate judicial decisions that have applied the law in a reasonable manner. It would be unreasonable for a change in jurisprudential understanding on a given subject to justify the assertion that a judgment prior to this new understanding had offended the legal system, giving rise to the filing of a rescission action.

Based on the arguments presented, it is justifiable to apply the wording of summary no. 343 to a final judgment, when the Supreme Court changes the understanding previously summarized, in homage to the principle of legal certainty represented by res judicata.

It is worth noting that the Supreme Court can restrict the binding effects of the decision or grant it effect from another time in the future, as long as it does so by a two-thirds majority of its members, as expressly provided for in Article 4 of Law 11.417/2006. In this case, the effects are extended to a future time.

The situation is different when the legislature repeals the law that is the subject of a binding ruling. In this case, it is not the Supreme Court that changes its mind, but the legislature. In order to avoid inconsistency, as is the case with many of the STF's persuasive summaries, article 5 of law 11.417/2006 determines that a revision or cancellation should be made, with the aim of adapting the court's jurisprudence to the new legislative reality.

In the event of the repeal of the law, the revised/cancelled summary will continue to produce effects for situations that occurred under the previous law. In the words of Glauco Salomao (200, p. 55), *verbis:*

> On the other hand, it could be thought that if a binding summary were not to declare unconstitutionality, then it would be affected by any subsequent law. Even so, one should not conclude that the summary is automatically prejudicial, because binding summaries, although they can no longer produce legal effects for future situations, will produce them to govern facts that occurred in the past, during the period in which they were in force. In these cases, the summary remains the parameter and basis of validity. Thus, the addressees of a binding rulings will have to apply the interpretation contained therein, from its entry into force, to the facts that occurred in that period and during the validity of the law on which the rulings were based. In other words, the rulings will be useful for continuing to establish the appropriate legal solution to conflicts that have arisen during the period in which they and the law were in force.

Therefore, binding rulings that interpret the law can be revised/cancelled both because of a change in the Supreme Court's interpretation and because of the repeal of the interpreted law. In this case, the revision of the summary is a logical consequence of the repeal of the law, since the accessory (summary) follows the principal (law). The consequences are the same as for the repeal of the law, i.e. it will have effect against all and *ex nunc.*

CONCLUSION

In this study, after analyzing some aspects relating to the institute of res judicata, the binding summary and the effects of its revision or cancellation on res judicata, in the light of Constitutional Amendment n. 45/2004, Law n. 11.417/2006, Brazilian doctrine and case law, it can be said that, if the system is well applied, it will bring important results in the realization of the rights of the jurisdictions.

As can be seen from the study of Law 11.417/2006, the binding summary is insufficiently regulated, as it is limited to defining the procedure without worrying about the consequences of its insertion, revision or cancellation. In order to complement this law, the Supreme Court issued two resolutions (Resolution No. 381 of October 29, 2008 and Resolution No. 388 of December 5, 2008), but they did not bring anything new.

Alongside the binding summary, the reform of the judiciary tried to insert a summary preventing appeals, but was unsuccessful in getting the final text approved. The ordinary legislator subsequently regulated the matter in the Code of Civil Procedure in such a timid way that it is incapable of producing concrete results. Given the magnitude of the institute, just one paragraph is not enough to make it effective.

As the creation of the summula originates in the judgment of repeated particular cases, but produces effects against all, along the lines of direct actions of unconstitutionality and declaratory actions of constitutionality, the Institute can be identified as being of a mixed nature, i.e. it presents characteristics of the diffuse-concrete model and the abstract-concentrated model of constitutional jurisdiction.

In this context, it can be concluded that binding rulings that deal with the constitutionality of a law or normative act apply the rules relating to direct actions of unconstitutionality and declaratory actions of constitutionality. In this sense, once a summula has been created, it can no longer be revised or canceled, unless there is a change in the constitutional rule that served as the basis for creating the summula. If the constitutional rule is repealed, the Supreme Court must revise or cancel it, under the terms of art. 5 of law 11.417/2006, in order to adapt it to the new constitutional reality. The effects are *ex nunc, i*.e. they take effect from of the amendment to the text of the Magna Carta. Binding Summula No. 8 has these characteristics, *verbis:* "The sole paragraph of article 5 of Decree-Law no. 1.569/1977 and articles 45 and 46 of Law no. 8.212/1991, which deal with prescription and decay of tax credit, are unconstitutional." Therefore, it is not possible to bring a rescission action to set aside a final judgment based on the application of the revised or canceled summary.

In the same vein, if the repealed or canceled summary is concerned with the validity, interpretation or effectiveness of a specific rule, without declaring the constitutionality of a specific provision of law, the change does not give rise to the filing of a rescission action. In this case, the guidance of STF summary no. 343 applies, *verbis*: "No action for rescission for infringement of a literal provision of law may be brought when the rescinding decision is based on a legal text whose interpretation is controversial in the courts." Now, if the Federal Supreme Court has summarized an understanding in one sense and then revised or canceled it, it is more than proven that there is current controversy. For example, if the STF's Binding Summary No. 5 is revised to apply the understanding that the lack of a technical defense by a lawyer in disciplinary administrative proceedings renders the proceedings null and void, this revised summary will not affect final judgments based on the current content of Summary No. 5, *verbis:* "The lack of technical defense by a lawyer in disciplinary administrative proceedings does not offend the Constitution."

Similarly, if the law interpreted by a binding precedent is repealed, the precedent must be brought into line with the new law. In this case, there is no need to talk about retroactive effects of the new ruling, since the previous law was valid and effective.

Therefore, unlike the creation of a binding summary, its revision or cancellation in all cases produces *ex nunc* effects. What changes is only the basis, depending on the reason for the revision or cancellation.

REFERENCES

ALEGRE, Jose Sergio Monte. *Binding Sumulas: are they the fruit of a poisoned tree?* Jus Navigandi, Teresina, year 13, n. 2009, December 31, 2008. Available at: <http://jus2.uol.com.br/doutrina/texto.asp?id=12148>. Accessed on: April 09, 2009.

BRANCO, Janaina Soares Noleto Castelo. *Sumula vinculante in the context of the Brazilian system of constitutionality control.* Available at: http://www.ffb.edu.br/_download/Dialogo_Juridico_n6_10.PDF. Accessed on: April 09, 2009.

BRAZIL, Federal Senate. *Binding effect.* Brasilia, DF, 1999.

BRAZIL. Constitution. *Federal Constitution of the Federative Republic of Brazil of 1988.*

BRAZIL. *Law 11.417/2006.* Regulates the binding summary.

CORTES, Osmar Mendes Paixao. *Sumula Vinculante e Seguranga Juridica.* Sao Paulo: Revista dos Tribunais, 2008.

DAIDONE, Decio Sebastiao. *A Sumula Vinculante e Impeditiva.* Sao Paulo: LTr, 2006.

DINAMARCO, Candido Rangel. *Institutions of Civil Procedural Law. Vol. III.* 3ª Ed. Sao Paulo: Malhoiros, 2003.

FIGUEIREDO, Leonardo Vizeu. *Sumula vinculante e a Lei n. 11.417/2006: apontamentos para compreensão do tema.* Jus Navigandi, Teresina, year 11, n. 1295, 17 Jan. 2007. Available at: http://jus2.uol.com.br/doutrina/texto.asp?id=9400. Accessed on: April 09, 2009.

FREITAS, Marcio Vieira. *Considerations on the so-called "binding sumula".* Jus Navigandi, Teresina, year 9, n. 503, November 22, 2004. Available at: <http://jus2.uol.com.br/doutrina/texto.asp?id=5969>. Accessed on: April 9, 2009.

GOMES, Luiz Flavio. *Sumulas vinculantes.* Jus Navigandi, Teresina, year 11, n. 1296, 18 Jan. 2007. Available at: <http://jus2.uol.com.br/doutrina/texto.asp?id=9402>. Accessed on: April 14, 2009.

GOUVEIA, Alessandro Samartin de. *Sumula vinculante e resolugao do Senado: crise na separação dos poderes?* Available at: http://www.netlegis.com.br/indexRC.jsp?arquivo=detalhesArtigosPublicados.jsp&cod2=851. Accessed on: April 9, 2009.

HARTMANN, Rodolfo Kronemberg. *A sumula vinculante e a lei 11.417/06.*Available at: http://www.jfrj.gov.br/Rev_SJRJ/num20/artigos/artigo_04.pdf. Accessed on: April 09, 2009.

IURK, Cassiano Luiz. *Coisa Julgada e Seguranga Juridica: Interrelagoes entre o*

Classico e o Novo. Curitiba: JM Livraria Juridica, 2008

JANINI, Alexandre. *Sumula vinculante and the language of law.* Available at: www.facape.br/anderson/ied2/Sumula_vinculante_e_a_linguagem_do_direito.doc -. Accessed on: April 09, 2009.

LEITE, Glauco Salomao. *Sumula Vinculante e Jurisdigao ConstitucionalBrasileira.* Rio de Janeiro: Biblioteca Forense Digital 2.0, 2007.

LENZA, Pedro. *Direito Constitucional Esquematizado. 12ª Ed. rev., atual. e ampl.* Sao Paulo: Saraiva, 2008.

LOBO, Arthur Mendes. *Brief Comments on the Regulation of the Binding Summula.* Available at: http://revistajuridica.fafibe.br/arquivos/breves_comentarios_sobre_a_regulamentacao_da.pdf. Accessed on: April 09, 2009.

MARINONI, Luiz Guilherme. *Coisa Julgada Inconstitucional: a retroatividade da decisão de (in)constitucionalidade do STF sobre a coisajulgada: a questão da relativização da coisa julgada.* Sao Paulo: Revista dos Tribunais, 2008

MENDES, Gilmar Ferreira, *et. al. Constitutional Law Course. 4ª* ed., ver. and current. Sao Paulo: Saraiva, 2009.

MENDES, Gilmar. *The binding effect of the decisions of the Federal Supreme Court in cases of abstract control of norms.* Jus Navigandi, Teresina, year 4, n. 43, jul. 2000. Available at: <http://jus2.uol.com.br/doutrina/texto.asp?id=108>. Accessed on: April 14, 2009.

NERY, Rosa Maria de Andrade; NERY JUNIOR, Nelson. *Codigo de Processo Civil Comentado e Legislagao Extravagante. 10th Ed. Rev., Ampl. e atual.* Sao Paulo: Revista dos Tribunais, 2007.

RAMOS, Andre Luiz Santa Cruz. *Coisa Julgada Inconstitucional.* Bahia: Podivm, 2007.

SGARBOSSA, Luis Fernando; JENSEN, Geziela. *Constitutional Amendment no. 45/04, the binding summa and the magistrate's free will. A brief essay on hypotheses of inapplicability.* Jus Navigandi, Teresina, year 9, n. 708, June 13, 2005. Available at: <http://jus2.uol.com.br/doutrina/texto.asp?id=6884>. Accessed on: April 14, 2009.

SILVA, Bruno Mattos e. *The binding summary for the Public Administration approved by the Reform of the Judiciary* . Jus Navigandi, Teresina, year 9, n. 541, December 30, 2004. Available at: <http://jus2.uol.com.br/doutrina/texto.asp?id=6101>. Accessed on: April 14, 2009.

TAVARES, Andre Ramos. *New Binding Summula Law: studies and comments on Law 11.417, of December 19, 2006.* Sao Paulo: Metodos, 2007.

TAVARES, Andre Ramos. *Perplexity of the New Institute of the Binding Ruling in Brazilian Law.* Electronic Journal of State Law. N. 11, July/August/September 2007. Salvador - Bahia - Brazil. Available at:

http:ZZrevistajuridica.fafibe.br/arquivos/breves_comentarios_sobre_a_regulamentacao _da.pdf. Accessed on April 9, 2009.

THEODORO JUNIOR, Humberto. *Course in Civil Procedural Law. Vol. I.* 41ª Ed, Rio de Janeiro: Forense, 2004.

MIX
Papier aus verantwortungsvollen Quellen
Paper from responsible sources
FSC® C105338

Printed by Books on Demand GmbH, Norderstedt / Germany